Worthless men
Race, eugenics and the death penalty
in the British Army
during the First World War

Gerard Oram teaches at the University of
Hertfordshire. He has been researching the use of
the death penalty in the military for a number of
years and he is continuing to research military
executions with the assistance of a grant from
the Open University. He is the author of
*Death Sentences Passed by Military Courts of the
British Army 1914–1924*. He lives in
Buckinghamshire with his wife, Anna.

Clive Emsley is Professor of History at the
Open University. He is currently President of
the International Association for the History of
Crime and Criminal Justice.He has taught at
universities in Calgary, Brisbane and Paris. He is the
author of *Crime and Society in England
1740–1900*, *The English Police: A Political and
Social History* and *Gendarmes and the State in
Nineteenth Century Europe*.

D1291540

Gerard Oram

Worthless men
Race, eugenics and the death penalty in the British Army during the First World War

With a foreword by Clive Emsley

Francis
Boutle
Publishers

First published by Francis Boutle Publishers
23 Arlington Way
London EC1R 1UY
(0171) 278 4497

ISBN 0 9532388 3 0

Printed in Great Britain by Redwood Books

Acknowledgements

I am most grateful to the Trustees of the Imperial War Museum for allowing me access to archive material and for permission to reproduce photographic material, and to the staff in the Departments of Documents and Photographs for their help and guidance. For permission to quote from the published work of Rudyard Kipling I am grateful to the National Trust for Places of Historic Interest or Natural Beauty and A.P. Watt Ltd.; for permission to quote from the work of John Buchan I am grateful to the Lord Tweedsmuir, Jean, Lady Tweedsmuir and A.P. Watt Ltd; for permission to quote from the work of H. G. Wells I am grateful to the literary executors of the estate of H.G.Wells and A. P. Watt Ltd. For permission to reproduce Wilfred Owen's poem '1914', I am grateful to the estate of Wilfred Owen, Professor Jon Stallworthy and Chatto and Windus Publishers. I am also grateful to copyright holders of private papers held at the Imperial War Museum for permission to quote from extracts; Mr Tony Maxse for the papers of General Sir Ivor Maxse; Mrs R.C.Ridley for the papers Lt. C.S.Rawlins; and Mrs A.White for the papers of Leading-Seaman Thomas MacMillan. Acknowledgement is also due to the controller of Her Majesty's Stationary Office for permission to reproduce Crown copyright material in the Public Record Office and to Earl Haig for his co-operation.

Every effort has been made to trace individuals for permission to quote copyright material in this publication. If I have inadvertantly omitted anyone to whom acknowledgement is due, I offer my sincere apologies.

Gerard Oram
November 1998.

Contents

List of illustrations

List of tables and graphs

Foreword

by Clive Emsley

The death penalty is an emotive subject and one about which it is difficult to be neutral. The execution of soldiers in the British army during World War One excites particular passion, partly because the abiding popular image of the war is one of senseless slaughter. This book sets out to explain why these executions happened; and perhaps the point needs to be emphasized at the outset, while some people, and not least some politicians, confuse the two words, explanation is not a synonym for excusal.

The subject of this book is essentially military, but the approach is broadly that of the social historian and parallels some of the issues that are currently the focus of research by historians of crime and criminal justice. Military history has long been a popular sub-discipline in its own right, but armies can never be entirely isolated from the societies from which they are drawn. Similarly, although some jurists tend to enshrine the Law as an organic entity somehow existing above society, laws remain things created by individual people in a particular context, and enforced by others in changing contexts. The functionaries who enforce laws cannot but bring to their activities the cultural baggage, including prejudices, of the society in which they work. It may not be comfortable to find that decisions about which men to execute and which to reprieve appear to have been made on eugenicist or racial grounds, yet it is important to be aware of the probability. At the same time, however, such an awareness should not be taken as the opportunity for condemning the military of 1914 to 1918 for not having the aspirations and morality of a contemporary, multicultural society.

In addition to explaining the decisions of courts martial and the High Command, tangentially this book raises other significant issues about the development of modern Britain. During the eighteenth century England had a notorious 'Bloody Code' under which the principle punishment for felony was death. Reform of the criminal law, most notably during the 1820s, largely limited the death penalty to homicide offences yet proportionately, Victorian Britain, which prided itself on its progress, morality and liberalism, appears to have executed more offenders than its continental neighbours – and this in spite of the fact that, according to the homicide statistics, murder was less common in Britain than in many other European countries. The drum-head courts martial which followed the Paris Commune of 1871 saw army officers making decisions on their perceptions of prisoners and whether or not they belonged to the 'dangerous classes'. Yet, half a century later, and even in the aftermath of the serious mutinies of 1917, the French army appears to have taken a more lenient line with offenders than its British ally. Imperial Germany executed fewer offenders, and, during the First World War, the Imperial German Army executed fewer of its soldiers. The British army's predilection for shooting offenders thus appears to have followed the pattern detectable in civil society, but why a society which prided itself on its progress, and on escaping both the revolutions of nineteenth century France and the militarism of Imperial Germany should have felt the need to employ the death penalty as often as it did remains an open question.

Such musings take us some way from the subject matter of this book. However, they emphasize the importance of historians developing links between their specialisms and also with other disciplines. Military history, social history, the history of criminal justice, intersect in what follows to provide a better understanding of a tragic and, to many eyes, inglorious aspect of World War One, but also to highlight other, important issues about the broader history of British society.

Preface

Why another book about executions in the First World War? Other authors have published detailed accounts of the trials and even, in some cases, the background of the executed soldiers. There has even been a government inquiry into the question of issuing pardons to those who were shot at dawn. What all this probing has made manifest is a deep concern with justice, but though I too would like to see justice done, I do believe that too exclusive an emphasis on redressing wrongs narrows our understanding of how the death penalty was applied by the British Army.

Quite naturally, writers have focused on cases where injustice appears most obvious. Whenever the executions become newsworthy, as was recently the case, the newspapers invariably highlight the same dozen or so cases. I do not wish to detract from the seriousness of these cases, but there is a danger of ignoring the other, less newsworthy, ones. Only by assessing all the available information can we come close to an understanding of this particular chapter in the history of the First World War, and that means including in our analyses men who simply deserted for no apparent reason other than self-preservation. Some men, in point of fact, were guilty of serious crimes – though few nowadays would argue that they deserved to be shot. For the serious historian their cases are every bit as important as any others.

The huge numbers of death sentences passed by courts martial, but which were not carried out have been largely neglected by other writers. True, only the barest details about these cases are available, yet sufficient data has survived to enable us to identify who these people were and when and where they were convicted. In most other areas historians would feel spoilt to have so much primary material to work with. But we need now to look critically at the bigger picture. The death penalty should be placed within the context of the army as an institution, the nature of the First World War and, attitudes in British society. Equally importantly, we need to examine how Britain's deployment of large numbers of troops and labourers from the Empire brought assumptions about race into the foreground. Only by fully contextualising can we write a true history of military executions.

My own feelings about pardons for the executed soldiers are coloured by my abhorrence at the very existence of a death penalty. Perhaps this is why I find no problem including in my analysis those who were executed for murder alongside those who simply cracked under the strains of trench warfare. Once again, I would argue that if we are to understand the army's use of the death penalty then we cannot afford to pick and choose which cases to examine on the basis of the type of offence.

I consider myself a social historian rather than a military historian and this has undoubtedly influenced my approach. It seemed to me that the crucial question was what was so special about a relatively small group of men that they were picked out to be executed? It seemed to me that their crimes were, in most cases, no worse than those of thousands of others. Therefore I had to compare them with the cases of those whose death sentences were not carried out and then with the rest of the British Army. Needless to say this has involved some detailed statistical analysis, much of which is reproduced in this book.

Details of every single death sentence passed by the British Army during the First World War – and there were approximately three and a half thousand of them – had to be collated, computed and analysed. This became the raw material of my research and has already been published (also by Francis Boutle Publishers) as a separate book. The data was compiled approximately two years ago. This proved to be fortunate because in the summer of 1997 the government removed many of the documents from the Public Record Office in order to conduct its own review of the death sentences – a reminder that we cannot take access to public records for granted. The documents have only recently been returned. Fortunately, my notes were extensive and well organised – a salutary lesson for other researchers. The government review was concluded recently with the announcement that there would be no posthumous pardons issued to the executed soldiers.

This book, however, has not been written in response to the government's decision. It was first written as a MPhil thesis at the University of Hertfordshire in 1997. Since then some of my views have been further developed, but the basis of my argument and analysis has not altered. Some areas have been expanded upon and readers will be relieved to hear that there is less statistical analysis here than in the thesis version. I have, however, included as much data as possible in the comparative tables in the appendix for those, like me, whose misspent youth means that they actually enjoy poring over figures for hours.

There are a number of people who I wish to thank for their generous help with this project. First amongst these is Dr. Susan Tegel of the University of Hertfordshire, who supervised my research. The final result would have been a far poorer product without her expert guidance and help. My current research is supervised by Dr. David Englander of the Open University to whom I owe a similar debt. I would also like to express my gratitude to my examiners Dr. John M. Bourne of the University of Birmingham and Dr. Mathew Cragoe of the University of Hertfordshire. It is my hope that I have done justice to their suggestions and to their continuing assistance and encouragement.

Thanks are also due to Julian Putkowski who made his own archive available to me and whose encouragement never wanes. I am grateful, too, to my parents and to my children, Sara-Jane, Victoria and Christopher who have had to endure family holidays which incorporate frequent visits to battlefields, cemeteries and memorials. Last but by no means least, I owe a great deal of thanks to my wife, Anna, who has accompanied me to archives, assisted in the computing and even stayed up into the early hours checking reference numbers without complaint.

Introduction

Between 1870 and 1914 the British Army executed just three of its own soldiers. These included two Australian officers court martialled during the Boer War for shooting prisoners. From the commencement of hostilities in August 1914 until the armistice of November 1918, no fewer than 327 soldiers were executed by firing squad for purely military offences: 313 on the Western Front and the remaining nineteen in the other theatres of the war. Most of the executions (272) were carried out for the offence of desertion. Executions were also carried out for the capital offences of cowardice (14), disobedience (4), mutiny (3), sleeping on post (2), quitting post (6), violence (2), striking a senior officer (4), threatening a senior officer (1) and casting away arms (2). There were several more executions for mutiny carried out after the armistice. Other death sentences were passed for criminal offences such as murder, many of which resulted in execution. After the armistice, five soldiers and numerous labourers and muleteers attached to the British Army were also executed. In fact, by the end of 1920 the number of executions carried out by the British Army on men serving in its own ranks totalled 361, not including civilians who came under British martial law in places such as Ireland and Egypt.

Historians have produced differing statistics for the number of executions, depending on the source of their information.[1] Official statistics for the First World War often include the years 1919 and 1920, raising a rather fundamental question: when did the First World War end? Generally, the armistice date of 11 November 1918 is regarded as the end of the war, but this is a rather unsatisfactory, and for our purposes false, cut-off date. The war against Germany had indeed ended but the British Army's continued involvement in a number of operations overseas necessitated the retention of soldiers who might otherwise have been demobilised. An expeditionary force was sent to fight the Bolsheviks in Russia, while there was a continued British military presence in many parts of the world such as Egypt, Turkey, Mesopotamia, India and also in the modern day states of Armenia and Azerbaijan. There were executions carried out under the authority of British courts martial in all these places after November 1918. There was also, of course, an ongoing military commitment in Ireland. To ignore these events in a study of the British Army's use of the death penalty would clearly constitute a serious omission. In my previous book, *Death Sentences passed by military courts of the British Army 1914–1924* (Francis Boutle Publishers, 1998), I included all cases which arose from the First World War and, therefore, covered the dates 1914, the start of the war, until the army's use of the death penalty ceased in 1924.[2] *Death Sentences* is the only comprehensive survey of death sentences passed by British courts martial.

It is also my contention that while the emphasis remains on death sentences passed on soldiers for military offences we should not totally ignore the offence of murder in our analysis. Murder was punishable by death in the criminal code, therefore it was different to the other offences under consideration: they were purely military offences with no criminal parallel. Whilst conceding that murder was a very different offence to that of, say, desertion, I would also argue that many of the murders committed by troops were at least partially the result of the stresses and strains of warfare: most appear to have been drink-related or a result of grievances against senior officers. A central theme of this book will be the often inequitable treatment of colonial, or black, troops and labourers, looking at the imposition of the death penalty by courts martial in the context of ideas and beliefs about race and eugenics. For the same reason I would also argue that the executions of civilians – mostly Egyptians – must be included. There is, however, one notable exception to this: the executions carried out in Ireland after the Easter Rising of 1916. The events in Ireland have already been the subject of much debate and a study such as must limit itself to the impact of the rising on the treatment of Irish soldiers serving in the British Army.

The work of Babington, Putkowski and Sykes has done much to raise awareness about military executions. The thesis that executions were carried out to deter others has not been seriously challenged. However, other crucial questions now need to be considered. For example, British soldiers appear to have been more at risk than those of other armies: executions in the French and German armies were much rarer. Was this purely a result of the British war experience or are there more fundamental, structural explanations? Were some soldiers in the British Army more vulnerable than others? I would argue that there were: the Irish, blacks and those whose heredity was thought to be suspect were treated differently and more harshly than were others. To consider these points it is no longer sufficient to limit the analysis to executions. If we are to understand why some men were executed it is vital that we compare their cases with others who escaped the firing squad. Either their selection was completely arbitrary or it was underpinned by a rationale. I intend to show that in many instances such a rationale did indeed exist and that it was often defined by a mixture of disciplinary requirements and concerns about the character and heredity of individual soldiers.

Historians tend to agree that the total number of death sentences passed on soldiers by British courts martial was 3,080, the figure produced by the War Office in 1922.[3] My own research, which includes civilians and prisoners of war, has revealed that when these other groups are counted the total was in fact 3,342 with 438 executions.[4] Naturally, previous studies have concentrated on executions alone, with the result that the much greater number of soldiers who were sentenced to death but not shot has been neglected. Concerns about injustices have dominated previous work. While not denying that injustices did occur, it has to be admitted that there is little more that can be added to that particular argument. Therefore the broader approach, adopted in *Death Sentences*, has again been followed in this study: widening the debate to include the enormous number of death sentences in the British Army; scrutinising, probably for the first time, the reliability of the War Office figure of 3,080 death sentences.

The benefits of this broader approach are twofold. Firstly, it has the effect of broadening the study from 361 executions to over 3,000 death sentences.

Statistical analysis is therefore more reliable, as it is less prone to errors caused by possibly atypical short-term trends. Secondly, the role of the Commander-in-Chief can be examined in a wider context, for it was he who had the power to send a man to the firing squad, even though he only exercised it in roughly eleven per cent of the cases. What then does this tell us about the High Command of the British Army? In the majority of cases under consideration the Commander-in-Chief was Sir Douglas Haig, a person whose personal responsibility remains the subject of intense historical debate. Without entering into the wider arguments about Haig, the analysis of death sentences and executions does shed further light on his command. Haig's reputation as 'the butcher of the Somme' should be reassessed and the notion that he was in some way personally responsible for the execution of a large number of British soldiers is over-simplistic and superficial. Haig was a product of the army, its structures and its traditions. In so far as death sentences are concerned, it is instructive to compare Haig's record with those of the other Commanders-in-Chief.

Frequent use of the death penalty in the British Army was unique to the First World War: the number of death sentences and executions far exceeded that of any other conflict. The committee convened to examine military justice reported in 1919 that the death penalty had been properly applied and that its continued use was essential to the maintenance of discipline.[5] This rather superficial analysis of military discipline was designed to pre-empt criticism of the manner in which the death penalty in particular had been enforced. The committee, which comprised six politicians, five senior army officers and the Judge Advocate General, sat for only twenty-two days. Their twelve page report was short by the standards of the time. To what extent was this official explanation designed to reinforce pre-war procedures and structures? In this study we will address several key questions. Was the British Army's use of capital punishment as a disciplinary tool merely a reflection of the more general carnage of the 1914–18 battlefields, representative of desensitisation or cheapening of human life, or are there alternative explanations? What was the relationship between death sentences and the conduct of the war itself? Most importantly, was there any group of soldiers who were more likely to be sentenced to death by courts martial and what was the role of the Commander-in-Chief? As well as explaining the military justice system the death sentences are placed in the context of the progress of the war and the varying pressures placed on the army by events on and off the battlefield. The different theatres of the war are discussed and the character and diversity of the British Army is analysed with particular reference to the treatment of different ethnic groups.

Concerns about the iniquitous nature of the courts martial system and executions were evident during the war. The Independent Labour Party MP Philip Snowden, regularly questioned the Secretary of State in the House of Commons. The secrecy maintained both at the time and after the war probably served to heighten those concerns. Individual details were withheld and even the numbers of executions carried out were kept from all but a very select few. After the war, the number of executions was eventually revealed, but details of individual cases, including the names of the victims, were to be withheld for 100 years. The first files were only opened up to public scrutiny in 1989 when this period of restriction was reduced to seventy-five years.

The Labour MP, Ernest Thurtle, a veteran of the war who had been wounded in 1917, maintained pressure on the government during the 1920s. In 1924, he published a pamphlet, *Shootings at Dawn*,[6] which gave details of some executions. Although polemical in tone it is one of the few surviving sources of eye-witness accounts. Furthermore, it is itself evidence of the response of some former soldiers to the harshness of British military discipline. Thurtle repeatedly pressed the government, in the House of Commons, to reveal more information about individual cases and to reform the courts martial system. Some historians consider his motives political, and that it was the army itself that he was attacking rather than the death penalty,[7] but his contribution to the abolition of the death penalty for most military offences by 1930 cannot be over-stated.

In 1983, Judge Anthony Babington was allowed access to the courts martial files under the seventy-five year limit on the condition that he did not name any individual. He first published his findings that year in his book *For the Sake of Example*.[8] Details of cases emerged into the public domain for the first time, but not the identities of the victims. Babington argued that trials were often hurriedly convened and that junior, inexperienced, officers formed the panel sitting in judgement. Access to legal representation was rarely accepted by the accused and when it was it often did more harm than good, in spite of the presence of highly qualified lawyers in the army.

Julian Putkowski and Julian Sykes revealed the identities of those executed in 1989. Their book, *Shot at Dawn*,[9] also added much detail and background information together with full appendices, which made further research easier. Over the following years, the official records were gradually opened up to public scrutiny at the Public Record Office. Details of courts martial, including capital offences, were recorded in thirty-nine registers. Transcripts of each and every court martial were written down at the time. The file was then passed up the chain of command so that the commanders at each level could append their comments and recommendations to it. This system is discussed in more detail below, but the essential feature was the forwarding of the file to the Judge Advocate General's (JAG) Office for what amounted to a judicial review, to ensure the legality of the proceedings. After an execution was carried out the file was returned to the JAG's office and retained. It was these files which were made available at the Public Record Office in 1989, although the Ministry of Defence withdrew them between 1997 and 1998. It is principally from these two sources, and from the archives of the Imperial War Museum, that this study draws its material.

Some common issues run through each stage of the examination of the executions. The effect of shell-shock was the cause of much concern. After the war, it was widely thought that those executed for desertion and cowardice might have been suffering from that condition and therefore responsibility for their actions might have been diminished. A War Office Committee of Enquiry into Shell-Shock was convened after the war under the guidance of Lord Southborough to examine these anxieties. However, the effectiveness of a defence at court martial based on shell-shock needs to be assessed. Rather than excusing a soldier's flight from battle a shell-shock defence might have served only to draw the court's attention to the man's character. There was another group, it could be argued, whose responsibility for their actions might have been diminished, namely those under twenty-one-years of age, the then legal age of majority. Despite this, many minors were court martialled, often electing to defend themselves. At least forty-four cases involving minors resulted in execution. Miscarriages of justice, as highlighted by the works of Babington and Putkowski and Sykes, remain an underlying motif.

The death penalty was the ultimate disciplinary weapon available to the British Army during the First World War and its use has been the subject of considerable controversy and public concern. The number of executions may appear insignificant when viewed in the context of the greater numbers of casualties: the total number of executions was less than the daily average number of British soldiers killed in action.[10] Unlike the 'glorious dead', those who died without honour at the execution post were deliberately set apart, their cases reviewed by their commanders who condemned some and reprieved others. The process of discrimination did not cease after their deaths: even their memory was treated differently to that of their fallen comrades. Their names were not recorded in the casualty lists nor did they appear on war memorials in Britain. It is this process of selection, first by courts martial and thereafter by the various commanders, and the extent to which factors such as individual heredity and race influenced decisions, with which this book is concerned.

The British Army in 1914

Traditions, stuctures and military law

To understand how the death penalty came to be regarded as a vital element of military discipline we must analyse the traditions and structures of the army itself. The British Army in 1914 was dominated by tradition, but like other armies, it was undergoing a transition. The process had started in the previous century and then been accelerated following the war in South Africa in 1898–1902. Simply to regard the British Army in the First World War as old-fashioned and led by incompetent generals is to miss the point. The emergence of modern warfare tested every army, revealing inadequacies everywhere. All the armies involved in the conflict had to make adjustments, some more so than others. How each country dealt with the test of modern and total war largely determined the result of the conflict. In fact the British Army, like the national economy, eventually proved to be more adaptable than those of most other countries. The British Army, therefore, faced similar challenges and shared much in common with both allies and enemies, but there were some crucial features which singled it out.

On the eve of the First World War, the British Army was the only army of the major belligerent nations to be recruited on a voluntary basis. Other European countries had a long tradition of conscription, with the exception of the Belgians, who had traditionally recruited a small volunteer army and relied on international guarantors to safeguard national security. This changed in 1909 when the ailing King Leopold II agreed to the introduction of conscription. This seemingly unimportant point will assume greater dimensions later on in this discussion.

Abandonment of the voluntary principle as the basis for recruitment in 1916 brought Britain into line with the rest of Europe. It was a decision born out of necessity: the nature of battle during the First World War had had an immediate and direct impact. Warfare had become extremely soldier intensive and voluntary recruitment could not keep pace with the continual demand for recruits. Casualties, as is well known, far exceeded anything previously experienced and without intervention the army would simply have run out of men. The average daily death toll was in fact greater than the total number of executions throughout the war. In such a context the execution of a few hundred may appear to be a triviality. Indeed in a recent article the military historian Ian Beckett described the wartime executions as a 'relatively minor matter'.[1] However, the British Army obviously felt differently at the time: why else would it have gone to such lengths to convene trials and finally to execute these men? In truth the death penalty was generally held to be of vital importance to the maintenance of discipline and executions were widely publicised as a deterrent to others. The army took the death sentence very seriously and historians have a duty to do likewise. If there is little more to be added to what might be termed the judicial debate, there does exist a need for more historical analysis of the rationale that underpinned the use of the death penalty by the military authorities.

In early twentieth-century Britain, the service most responsible for the preservation of national security was the Royal Navy. Accordingly, the army remained a relatively small professional volunteer force. There were a number of reasons for this. Firstly, as an island Britain needed to be protected from any seaborne enemies. Secondly, there was the traditional aversion to maintaining a large standing army in Britain, which had its origins in the seventeenth-century. In fact there had not been a large standing army in England since Cromwellian times. Britain therefore enjoyed a period of some 250 years without conscription. Control of the army, however small in numbers of troops, had also been a traditional source of concern. On succeeding to the throne after the Glorious Revolution in 1688, William and Mary had to agree to sharing control of the army with parliament. This was intended to prevent any future monarch coercing parliament at the point of a pike as Charles I had done in 1641. The legacy of this tradition was a working class in Britain with little or no involvement with the army and the true extent of its loyalty an unknown quantity. Politicians doubted 'the working class's willingness to make "sacrifices" for the "common good" in time of war,'[2] a view shared by many in the military, a bastion of traditionalism. There was even hostility to Lord Kitchener's campaign to recruit a 'civilian army' in 1914.[3]

Lastly, Britain was an imperial power with a vast, widespread Empire to defend. This could not be achieved successfully without a large navy capable of sailing to any part of the world and controlling the sea-lanes. Accordingly, the Royal Navy was by far the largest in the world and British fear of losing superiority was an important factor in the naval arms race with Germany in the years prior to the outbreak of war. This concern was shared by military and political figures alike and was even the subject of novels, such as Erskine Childers' *Riddle of the Sands*. Written in 1903, his book warned of a potential German invasion via the North Sea.[4] Clearly, Germany had replaced France as Britain's most likely adversary in any future conflict, but the navy was still considered the most effective weapon against such a threat.

As a consequence the army was, through necessity, small but highly mobile. Most important was its capability of being transported to trouble spots within the Empire to maintain order and protect British trade, often in conjunction with local forces. However, the sepoy mutiny in India in 1857 had exposed the inadequacies of too heavy a reliance on native troops. Contemporary concerns focused on the loyalty and trustworthiness of black soldiers rather than examining the underlying causes of the mutiny. The result was a complete restructuring of the army, placing a greater responsibility for the security of British-ruled India on British troops. The one-sided memory of atrocities committed in the mutiny left an indelible mark on British consciousness and attitudes towards Indians. The savagery was far from one-sided, but the press and popular literature painted a picture of Indian savages murdering innocent British women and children by the hundred. Where the savagery of the British Army's response was acknowledged, it was excused as necessary or justifiable. Generally, the reputation of Indian soldiers suffered badly in British eyes although some troops such as the Sikhs and Gurkhas who had remained loyal to the British emerged from the incident with enhanced reputations.

These attitudes although formed in the mid-nineteenth century proved enduring and Indian troops other than Sikhs or Gurkhas were rarely trusted with artillery during the First World War.

It was, however, the late nineteenth and early twentieth century overseas wars that had the greatest impact on the army of 1914. The British commanders of the First World War had learnt their craft in the campaigns of the Sudan and in South Africa. The British Army of 1914 had been trained and equipped to fight a war of movement on the open veldt of South Africa rather than in the densely populated landscape of northern Europe, where large masses of troops could be moved quickly by rail. Thus in 1914 the British artillery in particular was comparatively lightweight yet highly mobile when compared to other European armies. The war in South Africa had a lasting impact on British artillery practice, most notably the addition of a shield to protect gunners from sniper fire. It could be argued that the introduction of the quick-firing field gun, which arrived with the French 75mm gun in 1897 (still in use during World War Two), signalled the dawn of modern warfare. The development of trinitrotoluene (TNT) as a propellant – adopted by the German Army earlier than the British – continued a process which burst into shattering reality with the firing of 820-kilogram shells from huge Krupp-built 42cm howitzers by German artillery at Liège in 1914. Equally importantly, the British Army had no experience of fighting against a highly trained and well-equipped enemy such as the German Army. Only the German Army possessed the truly big artillery pieces that would characterise the nature of war after stalemate had been reached. The British Army, and the French for that matter, had to catch up fast.

However, the impact of the South African war was not confined to the battlefields. The war in South Africa did more than any other single event to focus attention on the health and fitness of the population, with the physical deficiencies of military recruits causing great concern. Many felt that Britain was falling behind her continental rivals and would not be able to compete with a dynamic Germany. The scouting movement started by Baden-Powell was one attempt to improve the fitness of the British but it was not the only measure adopted or proposed. Nor were such concerns limited to Britain. Elsewhere the world order was increasingly being interpreted in competitive or Social Darwinist terms and military commanders such as the Prussian general Von Bernhardi were to the fore of this movement. The 'Imperial Crisis' in Britain, discussed in more detail in a later chapter, brought into focus disquiet about the fitness of the working class who filled the ranks of the army.

The only European war fought by the British Army since the Battle of Waterloo in 1815 was the Crimean War (1854–56). The tactics of Britain and her allies had owed much to Wellington and Napoleon but, as the American Civil War only five years later was to show, modern warfare was no respecter of tradition. The development of long-range weaponry and high explosive shells signalled an end to the concentrated infantry attacks of earlier times. The Franco-Prussian war of 1870 brought some of those lessons home to the participants, but these largely passed the British High Command by: its main concern after all, was the preservation of the Empire. The Russo-Japanese War of 1904–5 reinforced the lessons of modern warfare but, despite some British officers having witnessed the conflict at first hand, its implications were not fully appreciated. In particular the Japanese success had misled observers, who saw in it a confirmation that war was won by offensive rather than defensive action. Nor was the potential destructiveness of modern artillery fully understood.

The Empire did, however, provide Britain with much needed raw materials which would prove invaluable to her war effort. Not least amongst these raw materials were the enormous human resources Britain was able to draw upon. The British Army could recruit in almost every part of the world and no time was wasted in taking advantage of this huge asset. At the outbreak of war, soldiers enlisted from the dominions of Canada, Australia, New Zealand and South Africa and from the colonies in the West Indies and Africa. The contribution of the Indian soldiers, who numbered more than one and a quarter million, to the British war effort was enormous, but has rarely been fully acknowledged. Labourers were also recruited in China, Africa and India, providing vital additional manpower behind the lines and releasing soldiers for front-line duties. The role of the labour corps has often been overlooked and its contribution to the war effort underestimated. Labourers were to all intents and purposes treated like soldiers and were subject to the same discipline and authority as those in the trenches. They often carried out hazardous jobs under fire; some broke down under the strain and paid the ultimate price before a firing squad.

In pre-war Britain, recruitment was carried out on a local basis. Regiments were named after the counties where they traditionally recruited. This had replaced the previous system of numbering regiments and had the advantage, from a military point of view, of instilling pride in the regiment by inducing a stronger local identity. Regiments' nicknames often reflected their locality. For example, the Nottingham and Derby Regiment became known popularly as the Sherwood Foresters. The old numbers of the regiments were not lost altogether. Under the reformed system, regiments usually had two battalions, each approximately 1,000 strong when at full strength. The battalions were alternately posted to home and overseas service, normally India. Numbered 1st or 2nd, they were the descendants of the earlier numbered regiments. For example, the former 28 Regiment of Foot became the 1 Battalion, Gloucestershire Regiment and the former 61 Regiment of Foot became the 2 Battalion. The 28 and 61 Regiments of Foot had their own historical links to the county, having been known formerly as the Royal North, and South, Gloucestershire Militias respectively. This is typical of other county regiments, which made up the bulk of the infantry in the British Army in 1914. Regiments of Guards had their own histories and traditional recruitment areas, hence the Scots, Irish and Welsh Guards. Preserving such links had another advantage beyond that of mere rationalisation. Along with the structure of the old units the new battalions inherited their traditions and, most importantly, their history. The Gloucestershire Regiment displayed a sphinx on its cap badge to identify the regiment with a stand made by the 28 Regiment of Foot at Alexandria in 1801. Similar stories applied to other regiments and former battle honours were proudly displayed on the colours of each and every county regiment and recruits would be instructed in the details of former glories. This enhanced loyalty and promoted *esprit de corps*.

Tradition therefore, was an important and indispensable feature of the British Army. Indeed, it would not be an exaggeration to suggest that the army relied on its traditions for much of its structure and organisation. Regimental pride was a potent tradition that gave the army much of its fighting mettle and was an invaluable aid to the maintenance of discipline. Loyalty bound the private soldier in many ways. He was expected to be loyal to his country and to the army. He was also required to be loyal to his regiment and its commanders, but probably the most pervasive form of loyalty was that felt between comrades. This was partly a product of the local nature of each unit and partly due to the prestige inherited from each regimental history.

Four infantry battalions, each commanded by a colonel, made up a brigade, under the command of a brigadier-general. Three infantry brigades, together with an additional battalion of pioneers, made up a division, commanded by a major-general. The division was the basic unit of military administration. Deployment of the army was normally by division; it travelled by division; it fought as a division. In 1914, a division numbered approximately 13,000 officers and men, when at full strength. Needless to say, a division was rarely at full strength because of sickness and other manpower demands. This was before any battle casualties had been suffered.

Cavalry, too, had its own local and historical character, which usually acknowledged its original benefactor, such as the 3 (Prince of Wales's) Dragoon Guards or 4 (Royal Irish) Dragoon Guards. The Royal Scots Greys were the 2 Dragoons, the Inniskillings the 6 Dragoons, and so on. Counties also raised their own volunteer mounted troops known as Yeomanry and these too normally bore the county name. Cavalry regiments were divided into four squadrons, each numbering approximately 180 officers and men, except for household cavalry regiments (three in total), which had around 110.

The artillery was not identified in quite the same manner and was generally known by a battery number. These batteries belonged either to Royal Field or Horse Artillery. The main weaponry of these units in 1914 consisted of thirteen and eighteen pound guns and the four and a half-inch howitzers. There was also a mountain battery, an indication of the type of warfare anticipated in the defence of the Empire. The Royal Garrison Artillery, which normally operated larger guns supplied other batteries. Naval-style guns, larger and heavier, such as the 4.7 inch gun constituted a siege-train. The army also had a number of 5 and 6 inch howitzers on trial. In the summer of 1914 the army was testing a 9.2 inch howitzer although its use was still envisaged in traditional terms: 'most people believed that there would be few opportunities to deploy such a monster in modern war, unless a full-scale siege developed'.[5] After 1914, as the British generals learned from the experience of modern war, the artillery underwent significant change. A trench mortar battery was added and the numbers and calibre of weaponry available to the other units were increased.

The army was organised into an order of battle when engaging the enemy. Three infantry divisions, together with three cavalry squadrons and nine artillery batteries made up one army corps. Three corps made up an army, commanded by a general. In 1914, the British Expeditionary Force (BEF) was made up of two corps, which grew to five armies by the end of the war. Initially, the BEF was handicapped by a lack of cohesion between its component parts: generals regarded the infantry, cavalry and artillery as three distinctly separate elements with defined roles. Coordination and co-operation was hampered by the lack of mutual understanding. It has been argued that integration of the artillery proved to be particularly difficult for many British generals.[6] By 1918, however, the British Army under Haig's command had learnt much and become a far more cohesive fighting force and the allied advance at the end of 1918 owed much to this.

The command of the British Army was also steeped in tradition and was characterised by a personalised structure of leadership. Promotion was based on a system of protector-protégé.[7] Haig, for example, was 'adopted' by both Kitchener and Lord Esher (not to mention the King), and also enjoyed the support of Sir John French, particularly after the well-publicised incident when he loaned French a considerable sum of money. Haig in turn championed the careers of other officers under his command. The key to high command positions, it appears, was to be in the right clique[8] and by 1914 almost all of the very top positions were filled by cavalry officers. In common with other British institutions the army had its elites. The most senior officers, traditionally drawn from the upper echelons of society, had all attended a handful of exclusive schools such as Eton, Harrow and Winchester.

The effect of this was to distance officers from their charges and was apparent at various levels. The social divide, which distanced even a subaltern from the other ranks, was often upheld on the battlefield. Higher up the army hierarchy, the problem actually worsened. Social status, it has been argued, was related so closely to rank that after the start of hostilities there was little contact between officers above the rank of colonel and the rankers in the trenches. Some historians have argued that the High Command at GHQ became dangerously remote from subordinate commanders. Consequently, the Commander-in-Chief rarely understood the reasons for failure, which were often attributed by the High Command to poor soldiering.[9] Others have laid the blame for the supposed failures of command on more practical problems, such as poor communications. Before the First World War British generals were usually able to command their relatively small armies by giving verbal or written commands which were acted upon immediately. By the time of the Second World War radio communications performed the same function, but during the First World War the armies had become too large to command directly and radio communications were not sufficiently advanced to control them adequately from a distance. Just as it took an inordinate amount of time for an order to arrive at its destination, so too did it take a long time for information to arrive back at the command post. John Terraine has argued that without 'voice control' of their armies 'generals, in fact, became quite impotent at the very moment when they would expect and be expected to display their greatest proficiency'.[10] The problem was rooted not so much in incompetence on the part of individuals as in a structure whereby the social hierarchy of society was imported into the army, and compounded by the failings of technology. With circumstances placing both soldier and general in unenviable positions, the impact on morale and discipline was invariably negative. We will consider the implications in later chapters.

The small expeditionary force deployed in Belgium in 1914 was commanded by Sir John French and numbered almost 100,000. It was divided into two corps which later became armies; the First Army was under the command of General Sir Douglas Haig and General Sir Horace Smith-Dorrien commanded the Second Army. In an often quoted order the German Kaiser allegedly described this force as a 'contemptible little army'[11] Veterans of the first exchanges with the Germans, proudly adopted the nickname of 'the old contemptibles.' Their first contact with the enemy came at Mons, on 22 August 1914. A small-scale encounter involving the Royal Irish Dragoon Guards gave way to an intense struggle as the Germans attempted to cross the Mons–Conde canal. The inadequacy of the British artillery, compared to the German batteries, soon became apparent. However, the firepower of the British infantry appeared to have taken the enemy by surprise and German casualties were high. Nevertheless, the sheer weight of the German advance forced the outflanked British Army to retreat.

These first battles and the tortuous retreat took their own toll and the small British force was tested to the full. Lapses of discipline brought on by the strain of the early encounters with the Germans resulted in numerous courts martial, which showed an immediate willingness to pass the death sentence for a range of offences. On 23 August 1914, just one day after the first contact with the enemy at Mons, a court martial sentenced a soldier to death. It has often been argued that the British Army stood out amongst those engaged in the First World War because of its harsher policy on capital punishment[12], the early recourse to its use tends to support this view. The first execution was just the first of many. In fact, death sentences were quite common in the British Army and executions therefore greater in number. Before considering individual cases it is useful to make a comparison between armies, both enemy and ally, in order to explain how and why the British Army differed.

Britain's principal ally was France. Although official records of French Army executions are not yet available for public scrutiny, it is possible to extract information from secondary sources to illuminate this aspect of French discipline.[13] Unfortunately, the resulting picture is a rather confused one. Babington cites figures from the French army's historical department, the *Service historique* at Vincennes, suggesting that a total of 133 French soldiers were executed during the entire war, most of them as a response to the mutinies of 1917, which followed the failure of the offensive bearing the name of its planner, General Robert Nivelle.[14] William Moore supports this: he cites a variety of sources, indicating that the figures are, if anything, lower. Moore's sources give the total number of French executions as varying from twenty to fifty-six.[15] Guy Pedroncini has suggested that the official figures, quoted by the *Service historique*, are inaccurate and that records held at the *Archives de la justice militaire* show the true figure to be much higher.[16] He argues that before the mutinies of 1917 the President of the Republic had to consider an average of twenty-two or twenty-three death sentences each month and that the commutation of approximately fifteen of them with seven or eight executions being carried out was typical. A total of 554 death sentences followed the mutinies, forty-nine of which were carried out, according to Pedroncini.[17]

Confusion is likely to remain until the French records are opened to the public, but in any case, as the French Army was larger than the British, even parity would represent less use of the death penalty on the part of the French. Although France and Britain (including the Empire) each mobilised approximately eight and a half million men, the French put far more men into the field. This is reflected in the percentages of casualties: the French suffered 51.7 per cent casualties in battle compared to 44.4 per cent in the British forces. It appears, therefore, that whilst the number of executions in the French Army was greater than the official figure, it remained comparatively lower than the British total, despite the far larger French Army having to respond to a major mutiny.

Leonard Smith has further developed Predrocini's theme and constructed a compelling argument that the relationship between the citizen soldiers of France and the army leadership was of a political nature. The level of obedience and the nature of coercion of soldiers underwent a process of perpetual negotiation. Those executed after the mutinies of 1917 were selected arbitrarily to satisfy the army leaders, without serious objections from the ranks. Thereafter, the prosecution of the war was more in accordance with the wishes of the battlefield soldiers, for there were no more costly offensives.[18] Smith, however, probably overstates the strength of the bargaining position of the men in the ranks: Pétain was firmly in control of the French Army after the mutinies and the executions amounted to a demonstration of the strength of his position. A similar process of negotiation might have occurred in the British Army, but this remains an area relatively neglected by historians. Significantly, in the British Army the power to confirm death sentences lay with the most senior army officer and not with a political figure such as the President of the French Republic. Once again action in the field was influenced by structural features of the respective armies, in this case the political structures not just of the armies but of the societies themselves.

Records of German executions were destroyed in the Second World War and it is necessary likewise to extract information from secondary sources. Samuel Hynes gives the figure as forty-eight.[19] Richard Evans agrees with this figure adding that in total 150 death sentences were passed, which indicates that 102 must have been commuted.[20] Once again, it should be noted that the German Army was far larger than the British Army. Germany mobilised a massive eleven million men, 54 per cent of whom became casualties in battle. Moreover, unlike the British Army, the German Army as the senior partner in each of its alliances, bore the brunt of the fighting from 1914 to 1918. The British did not really take over that role from the French until 1917. Yet the total number of German executions was a fraction of the British. In fact, it was far more difficult to convict a soldier for desertion under German military law than under British law, with far fewer prosecutions being brought as a result.[21] The comparative harshness of British military law accounts at least in part for the relatively high number of executions of British soldiers.

This difference was not lost on contemporary observers. In an often-cited diary entry dated 21 December 1917, Prince Rupprecht of Bavaria noted:

The administration of discipline by the English is very rigid. Whilst on our side there is known to me only a single case in which a soldier on account of aggravated refusal of duty in the face of the enemy was shot, I gather from a compilation of the British orders which have been found, that at least 67 English soldiers have been shot under martial law in the period between 27 October 1916 and 30 August 1917.[22]

If anything Prince Rupprecht had underestimated the harshness of discipline in the British Army: the actual number of British executions during this period was higher, standing at eighty-one.

The American Army did not arrive on the Western Front until 1917 and played no significant part in the war until 1918. American military law had been reformed in 1916, a luxury not available to those armies already engaged in the war. This may explain why the total of American executions is only ten. There are, however, other factors to consider. Article of War 48 empowered the Commanding General of the American Expeditionary Force to confirm and order death sentences for offences such as murder, rape, mutiny, desertion or espionage. These sentences had to be approved by the President before being implemented.[23] In the event, the ten executions that did take place were carried out only for the offences of murder and rape.

Furthermore, the American Army exhibited a willingness to accept current ideas about mental conditions. By the end of the war, every American Army division had its own psychiatrist who, under American military law, was required to examine any man sentenced to death. In addition to the examination by the condemned man's own divisional psychologist, a further opinion concerning his mental state had be obtained before a capital sentence could be enforced. The British Army, like the psychiatric profession in Britain, remained hostile to psychological explanations, especially if they emanated from Germany.[24]

Traditionally there was also a greater tolerance of desertion in the American Army. During the American Civil War, often dubbed by historians as the first 'modern war', there was a remarkably high incidence of desertion on both sides. Historians have been able to show from compiled reports that on one day alone, 1 February 1865, the Union Army had approximately one third of its army absent and the Confederate Army was on that same day at less than half its total strength.[25] The military courts took a lenient view and assumed that absent men intended to return to their unit. Pleas of guilty to the lesser charge of being 'absent' usually resulted in dropping the charges of desertion.[26] Americans were also familiar from the period of the civil war with a form of battle stress known as 'nostalgia', a condition thought to be the result of a longing for home.[27] It should not be forgotten that the civil war had only taken place fifty years earlier (approximately two generations), and it was still within living memory that Americans had fought and killed each other. It is not unreasonable to assume that there was a lingering revulsion at the prospect of Americans executing their own countrymen. This would be consistent with developments in American society: before the end of the First World War in the United States there was a general rejection of the use of the death penalty. At the turn of the century, during the so-called 'progressive era', ten American states had abolished capital punishment.[28]

Figures for the Austrian and Russian armies are simply not available: there is little evidence to suggest with any accuracy just how many executions took place in either. In both the Austrian and Russian armies desertions appear to have been a major problem, but the experience of these two armies is not really comparable to that of the British: the war on the Eastern Front was a comparatively mobile war. Both the Russian and Austro-Hungarian armies suffered from poor communications and problems with the supply of equipment and food. This was a major factor in the breakdown of discipline in both armies, combining potently with political agitation. The incidence of executions in the Italian Army shows an inconsistent picture. Until the humiliating defeat at Caporetto in 1917 it seems that an execution was a rare occurrence. Thereafter, the Italian Army took a harsh line with desertion, which had, as in the cases of the Austrian and Russian armies, assumed enormous

Imperial War Museum Q 70742

Shamed but not shot: the American Army dealt with deserters in its own way

proportions. The eventual total of Italian army executions may be twice as large as the British. In the Belgian Army approximately 200 death sentences were passed and eighteen executions carried out.[29]

A direct comparison between armies remains a difficult issue because it is impossible to compare like with like. Not only were the experiences of each army different, but they were moulded by very different traditions. For example, there were more offences for which a British soldier could be sentenced to death than in other armies. This was in all likelihood the legacy of the retention of a volunteer army. The larger conscript armies of the continent had to maintain a structure that could cope with men who had not chosen to serve in its ranks. A degree of flexibility, tolerance even, had to be built into the system. In Britain this was not an issue and military law was less flexible, which naturally meant that death sentences were more common in the British Army. Comparisons between armies have to allow for these factors.

Conscription was the major difference between the British Army and the other European armies. The other armies, which executed far fewer men, all had a long tradition of conscription. Not only were they accustomed to administering a large army but they had to deal with men who did not want to be in the army at all. In short, they were well used to dealing with the problems of desertion and a general unwillingness to serve. Likewise, men of conscript age were accustomed to the idea of serving in the army. In Britain there was no such tradition. The British Army had traditionally relied on volunteers to fill its ranks and, whilst desertion was undoubtedly still a problem, the demands of a small volunteer army were very different to those of a large conscript army. In 1914 the British Army only recruited men who had volunteered and had therefore accepted the conditions of service. Although conscription was introduced in the British Army in 1916 there was no corresponding change in military law.

An army is often seen as a totally separate entity with no real relationship to society. This is a difficult view to accept; it is a product of society.[30] As previously mentioned, in Britain an elite few – all educated at top public schools – filled the very top positions in the army of 1914. Moreover, the army reflected the class-dominated hierarchical society of Edwardian Britain. Change was slow in what was essentially a very conservative institution. This was also reflected in the policy on discipline and punishment. One of the most common forms of punishment was Field Punishment Number One, which entailed tying a soldier to a fixed object such as a post or a wheel for lengthy periods of time. In the criminal code this would have been considered barbaric, but in the army it could be applied in seemingly trivial cases. Robert Graves recalled how his batman received twenty-eight days Field Punishment Number One for being drunk.[31] Military penal reform obviously failed to keep pace with developments in the criminal code.

It may be useful to pause at this point and consider how the administration of punishment in the criminal law in Britain compared to that of other European countries. In England and Wales during the period 1900 to 1914 there were on average twenty-seven death sentences passed every year, with an average of fifteen executions carried out. By contrast, in France, where juries could accept mitigating circumstances in order to avoid the death penalty, the figures were twenty three and five respectively.[32] Elsewhere in Europe the same trend can be found, with fewer states using the death penalty. Even in Tsarist Russia it was rarely used in criminal cases although, interestingly, there was less restraint in the Russian Army. In Britain abolitionists used comparisons with other countries to illustrate that Britain was out of step, describing Britain as 'the most merciless of Christian countries' and the criminal law as 'backward and unsatisfactory'.[33] In an article in *The Times* on 25 July, 1872 it was suggested that 'Italy is the country in all the world where people kill the most and hang the least, whereas in England they kill the least and hang the most'.[34] If, as seems likely, Britain had a stronger tradition of capital punishment than other countries it is not unreasonable to suppose that such a tradition could have existed in the army as well. This is an important point and one which separates Britain from the other belligerent countries during World War One. To summarise this vital point, in America and throughout much of Europe in the late nineteenth and early twentieth centuries there was a gradual move away from the use of the death penalty. However, this trend cannot be detected in Britain,[35] where at the time of the First World War there was a much stronger tradition of capital punishment, especially in the army.

I have argued that the army cannot and should not be regarded as totally separate from society in general and that wider social trends influence the administration of military discipline. This of course works both ways and should not be regarded as only a reflection of negative trends: progressive trends in society can also lead to similar developments in the army. This point is best illustrated by the American Army, where we can witness the influence of new ideas in psychology and the changing mood towards the death penalty in the nation generally. In Germany there was also a growing acceptance of these new ideas about the human mind. In particular, the case of Ernst Wagner illustrates just how far these ideas had influenced the criminal code and the medical profession. A mass murderer, Wagner had killed at least fifteen people including his wife and children. Despite an understandable public clamour for his execution, he was reprieved when the psychiatrist Robert Gaupp deemed him 'unfit to plead'.[36] It is unlikely in Britain at this time that this understanding of criminal paranoia would have been accepted. In this context it is worth noting the reluctance of the British Army to accept diagnoses of nervous conditions such as that which came to be known as shell-shock.

There is another obstacle to any attempt to analyse the different armies' approaches to executions, namely the number of summary executions which took place. An officer could carry out a summary execution simply by shooting an individual without recourse to a trial. Undoubtedly, this occurred in every army, although, in the absence of any official records, it is impossible to assess how widespread this practice was. Siegfried Sassoon recounts how he threatened two of his own privates with his pistol, apparently not for the first time, commenting, 'I seemed to be getting pretty handy with my pistol'.[37] A common rumour amongst British soldiers after 1916 was that the Germans chained some soldiers to their posts to prevent them deserting. In an unpublished diary, a British officer, Captain Schweber MC, describes how he discovered a number of dead German soldiers in a captured trench chained to a machine gun during the British advance of 1918.[38] This is more likely to be a misunderstanding of the harness system by which the Germans moved machine guns in the field, but the author clearly believed it to be a form of summary execution.

Diaries remain the only source of information concerning summary executions, but their evidence can be contradictory. A good example concerns the German spring offensive of 1918 when a massive attack centred on a part of the British line being held by the Portuguese Division. Under the onslaught, the unfortunate Portuguese broke and fled. What happened next is the subject of some controversy. In an attempt to prevent the rout and slow down the retreat it appears that orders were given to fire on both Portuguese and British soldiers by their own commanders. Brigadier-General F. P. Crozier claimed to have ordered machine guns and rifles to fire upon the retreating Portuguese.[39] At the same time, Lieutenant-Colonel G. Seton-Hutchinson claims to have ordered the shooting of approximately forty British soldiers who were surrendering to the Germans.[40] Edwin Campion Vaughan also recalled an incident during the Third Battle of Ypres when his unit captured a German bunker:

'As we all closed in, the Boche garrison ran out with their hands up... We sent the 16 prisoners back across the open but they had only gone a hundred yards when a German machine gun mowed them all down'.[41]

It is perfectly possible that the incident was an accident and the German machine gunner had not properly identified the target. However, it does serve to illustrate the sort of problems encountered when trying to single out examples of summary executions the true number of which will, therefore, always remain unknown.

Courts martial

There is very little that can be added to the work of authors such as Babington, Putkowski and Sykes concerning the structure, composition and jurisdiction of courts martial during the war. However, for readers unfamiliar with these works some basic comments would be useful here. There were four kinds of court martial available to the British Army in 1914. Only two of these had jurisdiction to hear capital offences and so we only need concern ourselves with them.

The General Court Martial (GCM) was the highest form of military court. Only the Crown or Commander-in-Chief had the power to convene it. A judge advocate presided and a panel of at least thirteen commissioned officers assisted him. This could be reduced to five officers if the court was convened overseas. In peacetime this was the normal form of judicial examination of serious cases. During the war a Field General Court Martial heard most cases, except those involving officers, which continued to be heard by GCM.

The Field General Court Martial (FGCM) was convened, as the name implies, close to the field of battle. It was obviously much easier to convene, requiring just three officers, the most senior of whom had to hold the rank of captain or above and who acted as president of the court. Any death sentence had to be reached by unanimous decision, but it was unlikely that in a disciplined organisation such as the army others junior to him could obstruct the presiding officer's wishes. Another feature, which distinguished it from the GCM, was the absence of a legally trained individual such as an advocate general, although this did change in 1916 when Court Martial Officers (CMO) were introduced. The CMO was a legally trained officer attached to each corps who attended trials to ensure legality. Almost all of the cases with which we are concerned in this study were heard by FGCM.

A 'friend' could represent the accused, although civilian lawyers were not allowed to practice in a military court overseas. On the rare occasions when the accused elected to be represented, it was normally by a junior officer from the man's own unit. Babington has argued that more use should have been made of the large number of well-qualified lawyers within the ranks of the army. He also suggests that representation, where it existed, did little good and on occasions actually harmed the defence.[42]

The power to try capital cases was derived from the annually renewable Army Act 1881. The 1914 version of the Act differs very little from the original: only a few words were altered, presumably to either modernise or tighten the language used – none actually altered the meaning of the legislation. It applied to all soldiers under British command, including Dominion troops (Canadians, New Zealanders, Australians and South Africans). The act also extended to colonial troops in the West Indian, Nigerian, West African and Gold Coast Regiments. The Indian Army was treated very differently and was subject to a separate Act. And though subject to the British Army Act, Australians were treated according to somewhat different rules. The Australian Defence Act did not permit the execution of Australian troops without the consent of the Governor-General, and then only for the offences of mutiny, desertion and treason. Despite many attempts by the British Commander-in-Chief, no such authorisation was ever granted. However, this did not prevent British courts martial from sentencing Australian soldiers to death, but the Commander-in-Chief was unable to confirm any of the sentences. Consequently, no

34

soldier serving with the Australian Imperial Force was executed during the war.

The autonomy of courts martial should not be overstated. In theory they had judicial independence, but it should be remembered that they too were part of a highly authoritarian institution. The British Army during the First World War was a highly efficient machine where little went unchecked by the High Command. Control of logistics and the organisation of such a huge force depended on this. The High Command received a constant flow of information about troops, morale, the state of various commands as well as information concerning the enemy, and the allies for that matter. Courts martial were no exception.

According to Gerald Hurst, a court martial officer during the war, the performance of the members of the court was often under scrutiny. Writing in 1919, he stated that courts were often pressured by convening officers (those who first called the trial, usually the unit commander) to be 'efficient disciplinarians', adding that 'no judge is free when his professional future is wholly in the hands of a convening officer'.[43] It was not uncommon for divisional commanders to circulate memoranda to express disapproval of leniency on the part of courts martial. In October 1917 the president of a court in the 42 Division had to submit a full written explanation about how the acquittal of two soldiers charged with plundering an empty shop had been allowed in his court.[44] Direct interference like this was probably rare, but this example does illustrate both the nature of the pressure that those sitting on courts martial could be subjected to and the degree of interest that commanders took in individual cases and matters of discipline. Needless to say, divisional commanders felt under similar pressure from corps commanders and so on. Each commander, at whatever level, would have been reluctant to be seen to be soft on discipline. All this created an oppressive atmosphere and might explain why in so many cases the courts martial passed sentences of death yet recommended mercy: it surely signifies a reluctance to pass the sentence which they knew was expected from them.

Of course it was natural that commanders took a close interest in the state of discipline in their units. Few incidents were more likely to draw the attention of senior officers to discipline than the loss of men captured in raids by the enemy. Clearly, this was not thought to be good for the morale of comrades. Such an incident occurred on the night of 29–30 December 1915, when a German cutting party entered British trenches and took nineteen men of the Northamptonshire Regiment prisoner. A court of enquiry was convened and it was decided to arraign two NCOs for cowardice. A report of the incident was submitted by the commander of 18 Division, General Ivor Maxse. In it he stated, 'I am therefore using the incident to illustrate to all battalions the necessity of never surrendering without a fight, even when caught in a hole'.[45] One of the NCOs, Corporal Tibble, was subsequently sentenced to death by court martial, but had his sentence quashed.[46] It seems likely, given the concern, expressed by Maxse that the court was made aware of the desire to inflict a severe punishment in this case.

Concerns about interference with the independence of courts martial were expressed by the Darling Committee in 1919. Although the final report was a highly conservative one which reinforced the status quo with regard to military discipline, one rare criticism did focus on the nature of interference with courts martial by senior officers:

'We are satisfied that during the present war officers have, in one or two instances, issued circulars upon the subject of sentences in terms which cannot be justified'.[47]

It was, however, only the *terms* of the circulars that the committee felt could not be justified. The publication of such circulars *per se* was accepted as 'necessary and right'.[48]

Sentenced to death

We were all of us provisionally sentenced to death in our own thoughts and if anyone had been taken seriously ill and sent back to 'Blighty' he would have been looked upon as lucky.
Siegfried Sassoon[1]

I could not look on Death, which being known,
Men led me to him, blindfold and alone.
Rudyard Kipling[2]

According to the War Office publication, *The Statistics of the Military Effort of the British Empire During the Great War 1914–1920*,[3] a total of 304,262 courts martial were convened (for all offences, not just capital ones). In 3,080 cases a sentence of death was passed. This figure, often quoted in studies of the executions,[4] is rarely questioned. It is, however, possible to assess its accuracy.

The army kept a record of all courts martial cases in a series of registers, now held at the Public Record Office.[5] These registers record the basic details of each case, such as name, rank, unit, offence and sentence. A total of 3,342 death sentences are recorded, 438 of which resulted in executions. These included a number of prisoners of war, along with 216 civilians (seventy-three of whom were executed) who were living under British military jurisdiction (details are contained in *Death Sentences*[6]). This shows that, if the number of death sentences examined is restricted to soldiers and labourers only, then the true number is 3,118. A further discrepancy exists if we use a third source, statistics compiled by Major Barnes of the Judge Advocate General's office for the War Office in 1921.[7] He gives the total of death sentences between 4 August 1914 and 30 September 1920 as 3,083, a figure comparable to the official one. However, it should be pointed out that both the official figures and those of Barnes were compiled in the 1920s and without the benefit of a modern computer. The official figure of 3,080 can be accepted as a guide only. Unless further data becomes available my own figure of 3,118, based on army records and then computed onto a database, must be regarded as the most accurate one.

An analysis of death sentences broken down by offence is now possible.[8] This can, in turn, be set into the wider context of the total number of convictions for each offence as recorded by both the official figures and Major Barnes, to give an indication of which offences were most likely to attract a sentence of death. The death sentence was liberally applied by courts martial: records show it being used as a form of punishment for thirty-six separate offences, together with several unspecified civil crimes.[9] However, its use was usually restricted to five offences in particular. More than two thirds of the death sentences passed were for the military offence of desertion. There were 40,000 convictions for desertion and in 2,004 cases a sentence of death was passed by the courts martial. Desertion attracted more death sentences than any other offence. Perhaps surprisingly, the offence of sleeping on post was next highest with a total of 449 capital convictions. Unfortunately, the official statistics do not differentiate between sleeping on post and quitting a post and give a combined total of 11,691 convictions for both offences. If we add on the eighty-two death sentences passed for quitting a post, the new total for both offences is 531. Similarly, forty-nine death sentences were passed, out of a total of 13,726 convictions, for striking a senior officer. There were 1,841 convictions for mutiny, fifty-five of which resulted in condemnation.[10] Finally, 439 convictions for the offence of cowardice produced 213 death sentences.

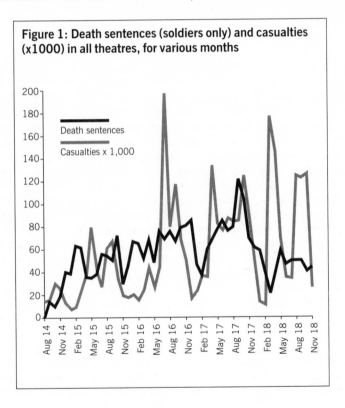

Figure 1: Death sentences (soldiers only) and casualties (x1000) in all theatres, for various months

What this shows is that the most prevalent conviction – desertion – was not necessarily considered the most serious offence by courts martial: only approximately one case in every twenty warranted a sentence of death. The ratio was similar for the offences of sleeping at or quitting a post – roughly one death sentence in every twenty convictions. Mutiny was even less likely to incur a death sentence, with only approximately one case in every fifty being considered sufficiently serious for the death sentence to be passed, and a mere one in every 300 cases of striking a senior officer attracted a condemnation. However, the offence of cowardice appears to have been taken far more seriously. Almost half of the men convicted of cowardice were sentenced to death.

This is a clear indication that courts martial considered cowardice the most serious offence: one condemnation in every two cases is a strikingly higher ratio than that of any of the other offences. The comparative rarity of charges of cowardice is a further indication of its seriousness. The courts treated the more common offence of desertion more leniently; the offences of quitting or sleeping on post slightly more so again. Surprisingly, greater leniency was shown to those charged with striking senior officers and mutiny. It is difficult to understand why the courts, made up of middle-ranking officers, should view the striking of one of their own (or of a non-commissioned officer) so lightly: surely this represented the greatest possible threat to their own authority. On the other hand it might have been *because* they were the victims of this particular crime that made them so reluctant to be seen to be tough on offenders.

The mutiny figures are rather distorted because most relate to the period immediately after the armistice of 11 November 1918. Some such sentences were still passed prior to November 1918, but not in sufficient numbers to match the numbers of soldiers who mutinied while awaiting demobilisation. The very reason for men being in uniform simply vanished after the armistice and the desire to return home clearly increased. The surge in mutinies immediately after the armistice can be understood in this context. It should also be noted that this analysis is restricted to how *courts martial* dealt with capital cases and it should be remembered that these courts usually comprised relatively junior officers, most of whom were serving at the front. Their concerns and priorities were likely to be dominated by practical conditions related to the front line and were not necessarily in accord with those of the senior officers of the General Staff, whose recommendations were ultimately more influential on the final outcome of each case.

There was also a relationship between the passing of death sentences and the progress of the war itself. With the exception of May 1915 and the whole of 1918, which we will briefly put to one side, Figure 1 shows that the number of death sentences passed gradually began to increase *before* the big offensives, identified by the huge rises in casualties. This indicates that there was a tightening of discipline by the courts martial before the big offensives and is particularly noticeable for the summer months of 1916 (Battle of the Somme) and the autumn of 1917 (Third Ypres), when the number of death sentences steadily climbed as the casualties soared. This is not surprising: one might expect offences such as desertion to increase at times of the greatest amount of danger and it was reasonable that the army would endeavour to maintain its fighting discipline through the courts martial.

The casualty figures, which include all theatres of the war,[11] illustrate clearly when and where the greatest action on the battlefields occurred. It can be seen that casualties rarely fell below 20,000 for any given month of the war – an indication of the prevailing manpower wastage of an army in the field. There are also a number of clearly discernible peaks when casualties rise dramatically higher than in other months. All but two of these peaks in casualties relate to battles on the Western Front. The first, in October 1914, was the result of the First Battle of Ypres when a British advance was checked by advancing German troops. This was effectively the end of a war of movement and for the following three years the fighting on the Western Front was characterised by stalemate. The next peak occurred in April 1915 and was caused by two separate actions. The first, the Second Battle of Ypres witnessed the first use of poison gas on the Western Front by the Germans (23 April 1915) and is usually remembered for the heroism of Canadian troops who stood firm to halt the German advance. The second notable action in that month was the first troop landings at Gallipoli on 25 April. There is also a peak in casualty numbers in August and September 1915. This relates to the Battle of Loos in northern France where the British Army first used gas. The offensive failed because the British were unable to capitalise on the gains achieved. Historians have long debated the roles of Douglas Haig and John French in this battle, especially concerning the deployment and positioning of the reserve. In terms of casualties and territorial gains the offensive was a disaster for the British which coincided with news of the reverses at Gallipoli and marked a turning point in public attitudes to the war.

In Britain 1916 is often associated with the Battle of the Somme, but there were other battles which we need to consider. As well as the huge battle which was raging at Verdun – resulting in enormous casualties for both the French and German armies – there was also action away from the Western Front. In April 1916 the British garrison under General Townsend surrendered to the Turkish Army at Kut-al-Amara in Mesopotamia (modern Iraq).The 14,000 prisoners, many of whom died in captivity, no doubt pushed up the casualty rate shown for that month. The beginning of the Battle of the Somme is clearly visible in the casualty figures. The offensive opened on the 1 July 1916 and the well documented casualties of that first day are the cause of the first great spire on the graph in Figure 1. In fact the progress of the battle can be traced from the graph: the casualties drop in the month of August and rise again in September, the second phase of the battle which was arguably more successful for the British Army. Casualty numbers then peter out, as did the British offensive during the approach of winter.

The two peaks in casualties during 1917 can both be identified with costly British offensives. The first in April 1917 was at Arras in northern France. This was the British contribution to the allied offensive planned by the French general Robert Nivelle. The British role was primarily one of diversion, but the capture of Vimy Ridge by the Canadian Corps was one of the great allied success stories of the war. Unfortunately, as the French offensive in the Champagne region collapsed in mutiny Haig was forced to continue his offensive to 'occupy' the Germans and take some of the pressure off the French Army. Casualties were high and little was gained. Similar considerations were a factor in the decision to go ahead with the offensive planned in the autumn of 1917 in Flanders, despite the poor weather conditions. The offensive, known as the Third Battle of Ypres, culminated in the battle for and capture of the Belgian village of Passchendaele. Figure 1 shows how casualties remained high for the duration of the battle throughout the autumn. It also shows that death sentences not only reached their highest number but remained consistently high throughout the period of the battle.

In 1918 there are two very large and sustained peaks in casualties. The first was the result of a German offensive in the spring, which broke the British line, almost achieving victory. The second was the result of the allied offensive which started at the Battle of Amiens in August and ended in the armistice of November. In both cases casualties were numerous and continued over a number of months, reflecting the nature of battle after the return to a war of movement. The German offensive of 1918 is particularly interesting. Death sentences actually dropped during this time, yet it was at this point, as the British Army fell back in a retreat which almost became a rout, when one might expect discipline to have been most rigorously enforced. Instead, the death sentence was abandoned, or at least suspended. Clearly, the army was preoccupied with stemming the German advance and had few opportunities to convene trials. It is also likely that summary executions were carried out. When the enemy advance stalled in May the number of death sentences increased. The Second Battle of Ypres in May 1915 was also a German offensive and once more, death sentences increased during the period of the battle rather than before it.

The death penalty, then, was most often applied during times of intense action on the battlefield, but in the case of British offensives the process of tightening up on offences such as desertion started before the battle.

Chronological Perspectives

The number of death sentences passed by courts martial increased steadily from eighty-five in 1914 to 591 in 1915. This was not just because 1915 was the first full year of war, compared to only five months in 1914, but the monthly average actually increased from seventeen to forty-nine. In 1916 the number of death sentences leapt to a staggering annual total of 856, or a monthly average of seventy-one. A similar figure was reached in 1917 when a total of 904 men were sentenced to death, a monthly average of seventy-five. The progressive increase in numbers of men condemned by courts martial between 1914 and 1917 can be understood as part of a general trend. The army had increased in size during this period from a total strength of 1,524,257 in 1914 to 4,760,788 in 1917.[12] With that increase came more military crime. Such an increase was natural and like any society the army must have anticipated this trend. The nature of the war had also altered: the war had ceased to be one of movement by the end of 1914 and the relatively small-scale offensives of 1915 had given way to large setpiece battles in 1916 and 1917. Casualties, a good indication of the army's fortunes, rose dramatically with these large offensives. The British Army had suffered approximately 99,000 casualties in 1914; 424,000 in 1915; 700,000 in 1916 and 836,000 in 1917.[13] The army had also undergone a change at the top during this period. At the end of 1915 Douglas Haig had replaced John French as Commander-in-Chief on the Western Front, where most death sentences were passed. The role of these men is analysed later, but it is sufficient at this point to note my contention that the death sentences were not determined by the will of one individual, however powerful he might have been.

The year 1918, however, is most significant. The trend of annual increments in the number of men sentenced to death was reversed, despite the army being larger than in previous years. Only 515 men were sentenced to death in 1918, a monthly average of forty-three. In terms of the death sentence, 1918 most closely matches 1915. Yet the army of 1918 was approximately twice as large as that in 1915 (almost five million compared with just over two and a half million men serving at home and overseas[14]). Casualties too, reveal huge differences between the two years. Indeed, casualties in 1918 (approximately 891,000) were higher than in all previous years. In this context, one might expect an increase in death sentences. However the number of death sentences passed in 1918 was almost forty per cent fewer than in 1917. Was this a reflection of the progress of the war, after all 1918 was the year of victory, or were there other factors which affected the sentencing habits of the courts martial?

The differences between 1915 and 1918 must be explained if we are to understand why there was such a massive reduction in the number of death sentences passed. The British Army suffered more than twice as many casualties in the final year of the war than in 1915 (890,922 and 424,305 respectively[15]). If there was a relationship between casualties and death sentences, as I have previously argued, then something significant must have happened to the British Army to upset the correlation in 1918. The reason for the reduction in death sentences in 1918 must be found in the altered structure of the British Army itself.

The army of 1918, as well as being much larger compared to previous years, was much more a conscript army. It is possible that the British High Command accepted a different responsibility to men who had been conscripted into the army and had not voluntarily accepted the terms of King's Regulations. This may also account for the reinstatement of the dependant's allowance for the next of kin of executed men in mid-1917. Previously, widows and other dependants of executed soldiers had not been entitled to any financial support. Public pressure may have helped the cause, but conscription had brought about a reappraisal of army and governmental responsibilities towards soldiers and their dependants, such as existed in France and Germany. It then took almost a year for this reappraisal of responsibility to filter down to the courts martial. Therefore, no change can be detected prior to 1918.

A comparison of volunteers and conscripts, which would assist enormously in this matter, is problematic. The appendix in *Shot at Dawn* shows the total number of conscripts executed to be twenty-six, a number significantly lower than the ten per cent for the army as a whole.[16] Further research suggests that even the figure of twenty-six might be an overestimate and the real number of conscripts executed, although not precisely known, is likely to have been far less.[17] The turning point in the army's use of the death penalty appears to coincide with the alteration in the army's structure.

This does not contradict the argument that death sentences were imposed in an attempt to firm up discipline in readiness for an offensive. Rather, the two explanations run side by side. In 1915 and 1916 the army was comprised entirely of volunteers, and it appears that the death sentence was applied as a pre-offensive disciplinary measure. In 1917, conscripts were beginning to fill the ranks alongside the remaining volunteers, but the army, always slow to change, retained the same approach. By 1918, however, things were different. Not only had the army altered, so had its approach to the death sentence. By the summer of 1918, when the British Army launched its offensive, the usual increase in death sentences is not evident. The subsequent success of this offensive cannot have been anticipated any more than before the offensives of 1915, 1916 and 1917.

The Court Martial Officers' presence at some trials may also have influenced the reduction in death sentences, but with only one CMO per corps the impact would have been minimal. It is also likely that by 1918 there was a greater understanding of the condition known as shell-shock, a subject we will return to. Again though, the impact of this would have been relatively slight, since most officers, including medical officers, still thought in pre-war terms: complaints of shell-shock continued to be regarded with suspicion. These developments amount to little more than tinkering with the system but it would have taken a fundamental change in attitudes, such as would have resulted from the introduction of conscription, to bring about a decline in the number of death sentences passed as large as forty per cent. However, the introduction of the CMO and the increasing awareness of nervous disorders did have something in common with the altered state of the army following the abandonment of the voluntary principle as the sole basis for recruitment. All were symptoms of the transition from a traditional to a more modern and professional army, which from 1917 onwards had increasingly more in common with the conscript armies of the continent than it did with the pre-war British Army.

Courts martial operated within the context of everyday operations. Discipline was a constant preoccupation of the army's leadership and was considered integral to an efficient army. The main disciplinary tool was the rank structure, which imposed the wishes of the few at the very top onto the masses in the ranks. Middle-ranking and junior officers were charged with the role of implementing this discipline at the front. If for any reason this broke down, recourse could be made to the army's judicial system, the main operational instrument of which was the Field General Court martial. As this was staffed by operational officers, usually of junior and middle rank, convened close to the battlefield, it reflected the disciplinary concerns of front line officers. The problems faced by front line officers varied greatly from those of the High Command. Front line officers were concerned only with their own particular section of the line and their experience was often limited to a very small part of the conflict. Senior commanders, who were expected to take a broader view of the war, were normally situated behind the front line. These commanders, whether at division, corps or army level had very different disciplinary concerns, and this was reflected in their actions.

Because of changing operational imperatives of the war at different times, responses to lapses of discipline varied and it is useful to divide the war into five stages, each corresponding to a calendar year, in order to facilitate an analysis of the changing demands made on the army.

1914: The first death sentences
The first death sentence of the war was passed on Private Whittle, serving in a regiment of dragoons. He was sentenced to be shot on 23 August 1914, the time of the Mons battle, for falling asleep at his post. The Commander-in-Chief, Sir John French, commuted the sentence to two years hard labour.[18] This particular offence was by far the most prevalent in that first stage of the war and is symptomatic of the hardship suffered by the men of the BEF during the arduous retreat from Mons. In all, thirty-eight of the eighty-five death sentences of 1914 were passed for the offence of sleeping at the post, although none were confirmed.

The first sentence of death for desertion was treated rather differently. Private Thomas Highgate of the Royal West Kent Regiment was tried and sentenced to death on 6 September 1914. On this occasion the Commander-in-Chief confirmed the sentence and a mere two days later, on 8 September 1914, the nineteen-year-old soldier from Catford was shot by firing squad.[19] The Commander-in-Chief had confirmed the first death sentence passed on a deserter referred to him. This, together with the speed the matter was dealt with, was an indication of just how seriously the High Command viewed desertion.

The next execution involved a twenty-year-old private of the Royal Berkshire Regiment. Private Ward was sentenced to death for cowardice on the 24 September 1914. Tried alongside Ward was Corporal V. Prior also of the Royal Berkshire Regiment; he too was sentenced to death. The Commander-in-Chief commuted Prior's sentence to two years hard labour and his rank was reduced. Perhaps the non-commissioned officer was valued more highly than Private Ward, whose sentence was confirmed. Once again, only two days lapsed before his execution on 26 September 1914. His was the sixth case of cowardice to have attracted the death sentence; the other five (including Prior's) were commuted by Sir John French.[20]

Another deserter was more fortunate. The Commander-in-Chief did not confirm the death sentence on Private Butler of the Royal Scottish Fusiliers.[21] Nor did he impose any other sentence, indicating that the conviction may have been unsatisfactory. The third deserter to be sentenced to death, Private Edward Tanner of the Wiltshire Regiment, was therefore only the second substantiated case of desertion to be considered for execution by Sir John French. The sentence was confirmed, again reflecting the perceived seriousness of the offence. Thirty-three-year-old Private Tanner was executed on 27 October 1914.[22] On this occasion, the execution took place fourteen days after the court martial, which is more typical of other cases during the war. The speed with which these first two cases were disposed of was rarely repeated during the rest of the war.

A similar fate awaited another man convicted of desertion. Twenty-six-year-old Private Archibald Browne of the Essex Regiment was sentenced to death on 9 December 1914. Ten days later, on 19 December 1914, the young soldier from Ingatestone in Essex was shot by firing squad.[23] Eight other cases of desertion had been referred to Sir John French in this period; two had not been confirmed (including the case of Butler) while the other six had been commuted to periods of hard labour or penal servitude. Two of those commuted cases involved infantrymen like Highgate, Tanner and Browne, the other four cases involved soldiers who, like the Commander-in-Chief Sir John French and his successor Sir Douglas Haig, were in the cavalry. Throughout the entire war not one single British cavalryman was executed.

Courts martial passed death sentences on eighty-five men in 1914. Four were executed; the remaining cases were disposed of in other ways. The Commander-in-Chief quashed some sentences, which suggests that they were unsound. Among them were the cases of James McNella, a driver in the Royal Field Artillery, who was convicted of rape on the 21 November 1914, and Private S. Martin of the Lincolnshire Regiment, convicted on 12 December 1914 of being absent without leave. It is likely that the latter was quashed because it was not a capital offence and the sentence therefore was unlawful. Another soldier, Private John O'Gara of the Manchester Regiment, was condemned to death for housebreaking. This conviction was also quashed, as were the sentences of two others convicted for sleeping on post. A sentence of death passed on 22 September 1914 against Private Chadwick of the King's Own Yorkshire Light Infantry for cowardice was also quashed, presumably for legal reasons. Similarly, there may have been problems with two other cases of desertion, because the Commander-in-Chief did not confirm any sentence at all. Six of the remaining seventy-five were confirmed and resulted in execution; the other sixty-nine cases were commuted to penal servitude or hard labour for periods of two to five years.[24]

One very unusual case was that of Private J. Stevenson of the 2 Scottish Rifles. He was convicted and sentenced to death on 26 December 1914 on two charges of being drunk. This was reduced to two years hard labour by the Commander-in-Chief.[25] There is no record indicating the circumstances of the offences but the proximity of the trial to Christmas might indicate that there had been a problem with drunkenness, which the court martial was eager to stamp out. Stevenson's case, however, was not unique: another three soldiers were sentenced to death for being drunk in subsequent years.[26]

From the relatively small sample of cases in 1914 we can see how the courts martial system worked. Some of its flaws are revealed, such as the lack of experience of the sentencing officers, who in at least one case passed an unlawful sentence. Paradoxically, this also shows that the built-in safety mechanism, designed to identify unsatisfactory convictions and/or sentences, had worked in at least eight cases. This safety mechanism relied on the identification of any problems, and was the responsibility of the Judge Advocate General, to whom all capital cases were referred. Flaws could also be identified by one of the commanders who appended their remarks and recommendations to the file as it ascended the military ladder, although this was rare. If any of these individuals failed to see the flaw then the case could end in execution. With no appeal court to act as a judicial examiner, the consequences of such oversights were very grave. Another feature of military justice was the speed with which cases could be disposed of. Undoubtedly the consequence of necessity and circumstance, it led alarmingly to the whole process being sometimes completed within two days. This, and the absence of any formal appeal procedure, constituted serious inadequacies in the courts martial system.

1915: Stalemate

The war in 1914 had been one of movement. The retreat from Mons had placed strains on the BEF, reflected in the death sentencing of the courts martial. After the Battle of the Marne and the construction of trench systems, the war of movement ended, at least temporarily. What was the impact of the very different demands of a war of stalemate on death sentences?

Sleeping on post remained an offence for which the courts martial were willing to pass a sentence of death. In 238 cases, men were sentenced to be shot for this offence. Even allowing for the relative differences between 1914 and 1915 (the war had only occupied five months of 1914) this represents a huge increase. Once again, however, the concerns of the Commander-in-Chief evidently differed from those of the operational front line officers on the courts martial and none of these cases were confirmed.

In contrast to the offence of sleeping on post, the Commander-in-Chief had regarded desertion much more seriously during 1914 and this remained the case in 1915. What had altered though, was the enormous increase in the number of death sentences passed for desertion, which leapt from sixteen in 1914 to 241 in 1915. More death sentences were passed in 1915 for desertion than for any other offence and the pattern of increase was replicated in each year for the rest of the war.

The very first death sentence for desertion in 1915 was passed on twenty-three-year-old Corporal George Latham of the 2 Battalion Lancashire Fusiliers on 11 January.[27] He had originally deserted at the Battle of Le Cateau in August 1914 but returned to his unit some weeks later, only to desert once more. He had been arrested in December after taking up residence with a French woman in Nieppe. His sentence was confirmed by French and eleven days after his trial Latham was shot.[28] It seems likely that Latham's previous desertion at Le Cateau was his downfall: sixteen other deserters sentenced to death in January 1915 were not executed. Private Lock, 2 Battalion East Surrey Regiment, had also been found guilty of forgery; his sentence was commuted to two years hard labour.[29] Two privates of the Royal Warwickshire Regiment had also committed other offences in addition to that of desertion. One had been convicted of cowardice and the other of threatening a senior officer and insubordination. Despite the seriousness of these charges both had their death sentences commuted to five years penal servitude.[30]

The numbers of death sentences passed for desertion were comparable to those for sleeping on post. However, the response of the Commander-in-Chief to these offences was not. Clearly, Sir John French took a more serious view of desertion than of sleeping on post. No soldiers were executed for sleeping on post in 1915 but forty-six convicted deserters had their death sentences confirmed. This represents a confirmation rate of nineteen per cent, identical to that of 1914. Other offences also attracted the death sentence in greater numbers. Fifty-one soldiers received death sentences for cowardice in 1915, a huge increase on the previous year by any standard. Four of these resulted in execution, a rate comparable to that of 1914. The number of death sentences for quitting post (seventeen cases) and disobedience (thirteen cases) rose; two were confirmed for the former offence and one for the latter.

The rise in the number of death sentences is partly attributable to the increased size of the army. The pattern of the offences for which courts martial passed a sentence of death reflected the changing nature of the war. Sleeping on post remained a major concern at operational level, but like 1914, it was not considered by the Commander-in-Chief to be serious enough to warrant execution. By contrast, courts martial regarded desertion more seriously in 1915 than in the previous year, reflecting similar concerns to those of the Commander-in-Chief. The number of death sentences for desertion increased dramatically from sixteen in 1914 to 241 in 1915. The Commander-in-Chief's response was consistent with the previous year and he confirmed an identical percentage.

Another influential factor in 1915 was the widening of the war to other theatres such as Gallipoli. Five executions for military offences were carried out in places other than the Western Front, three at Gallipoli for offences of quitting post, desertion and disobedience, one at Salonika for disobedience, and another in Cameroon for cowardice. Confirmation of these sentences was the responsibility of the Commander-in-Chief of the relevant expeditionary force. In Gallipoli, the responsibility fell on General Sir Ian Hamilton.

In many ways, the war on the Gallipoli and Salonika fronts in 1915 mirrored the stalemate of the Western Front, resulting in frustration at every level of the army. One symptom likely to have arisen from this frustration was the appearance of death sentences for the offence of striking a senior officer, an offence absent from the 1914 death sentences. Ten soldiers were sentenced to death for it in 1915; all had their sentences commuted. Three of these soldiers were serving in New Army units; the other seven were serving in regular battalions. Kitchener volunteers, despite the concerns of many senior officers, were no more likely to commit this particular offence than were regular soldiers. Therefore, the emergence of death sentences for striking senior officers does not reflect any disciplinary problem, real or perceived, within the ranks of the Kitchener volunteers.

1916: The Somme

When war broke out in 1914 Lord Kitchener, a national hero who had avenged the death of General Gordon at Khartoum, was made Secretary of State for War. Unlike many of his contemporaries, Kitchener did not believe that the war would be over by Christmas, nor did he believe that Germany could be defeated by the relatively small regular army of 1914. His scheme to create New Armies of citizen volunteers is still associated with the famous posters which bore his face imploring Britons to enlist. In the first wave of patriotism and escapism of 1914, many thousands of British men did just that, some forming Pals units based on local communities, clubs, associations and so on. Although some of these volunteers of the New Army had seen active service at Gallipoli and in the Battle of Loos in 1915, they came to be identified with the Battle of the Somme. The spirit of these citizen-soldiers was epitomised by the so-called Pals battalions, many of whom were slaughtered en masse on the battlefields of Picardy. Because of the manner in which they were often formed the Pals battalions were arguably the closest knit of all the army units and losses were harshly felt.

As the losses increased, so the bonds within the unit were slackened as the number of the original Pals diminished. This was a factor in the cases of Privates Longshaw and Ingham of the 18 Battalion, Manchester Regiment (Salford Pals). The two railway clerks from Salford had made their way to Dieppe and boarded a Swedish ship bound for England. It was an ill-conceived plan: any ship bound for England was scoured by the Military Police searching for deserters. The attempts of the two privates to pass themselves off as American tourists soon failed and they admitted their true identity when questioned. At the court martial Private Longshaw defended his actions:

My service on the Somme front had reacted upon my state of mind, which had become morbid and irrational, also the fact that *practically all of my comrades were gone* [my italics] induced me further to this act.[31]

Although less articulately, the sense of isolation felt by these soldiers was expressed more profoundly by Private Ingham, whose pathetic defence is reproduced here in full:

I was worrying at the time through the loss of my chums, also about my mother at home, being

47

upset, through hearing bad news of two of my comrades. I plead for leniency on account of my service in France of twelve months and my previous good conduct. I beg for a chance to make atonement. I left with my chum firstly to see those at home and then to try and get into the Navy along with my other brother, who is serving there.[32]

Privates Longshaw and Ingham had worked, enlisted and served together. They then deserted and were tried together and ultimately they were executed together on 1 December 1916. They were buried side by side at Bailleulmont Communal Cemetery where Albert Ingham's father had the following inscribed on his son's headstone:

SHOT AT DAWN
ONE OF THE FIRST TO ENLIST
A WORTHY SON OF HIS FATHER

Two men who had missed the Battle of the Somme, were the Bradford Pals, Privates Crimmins and Wild. A night of drinking left them by the side of a road in a comatose state. In the morning, when their comrades were dying in no man's land, they were absent. Despite a previous good record and one incidence of shell-shock experienced by Private Wild, a Bradford police officer before the war, the two Pals were shot on 5 September 1916.

There had also been a change at the top of the British Army: Sir Douglas Haig had replaced Sir John French as Commander-in-Chief. The Battle of the Somme was typical of Haig's approach to war: big offensives designed to break through the enemy line and achieve a decisive victory. Haig was aware that his plan would entail large losses and he realised that the nation needed to be prepared in advance. In June 1916, just before the offensive opened, he wrote a 'Memorandum on Policy for Press' outlining this view:

Together with patience, the nation must be taught to bear losses. No amount of skill on the part of the higher commanders, no training, however good, on the part of officers and men, no superiority, however great, of arms and ammunition, will enable victories to be won without the sacrifice of men. France, Germany and Austria have each lost in killed alone probably not less than one tenth of their male population capable of bearing arms. We must be prepared to accept great losses in future without flinching whenever and wherever it becomes necessary to sacrifice men in order to gain some important advantage or to foil the enemy's endeavours to gain one.[33]

During the spring months of 1916, the army also had to be prepared for the Somme offensive, which had originally been planned to begin on 1 August. Part of this process involved the tightening of discipline. Travers has shown how the army commanders were increasingly concerned about the discipline of their own troops as the date for the offensive approached.[34] The increasing number of death sentences passed before the battle commenced reflected these concerns. The Battle of the Somme began on 1 July because of the desire to relieve some of the pressure from the French defending Verdun, and in June death sentences reached their highest number. During the battle the number of death sentences passed dropped slightly before increasing once again afterwards.

More than sixty per cent of the death sentences passed in 1916 were for the offence of desertion – 528 cases out of a total of 856 – reflecting the courts' attempts to impose strict discipline on the volunteers of the New Army. A further seventy-nine death sentences were passed for cowardice. Sleeping on post had ceased to be *the* major concern of the courts martial: only 115 cases attracted a death sentence marking a major change from the previous two years.

The sentencing of courts martial reflected another change in the character of the army. Conscription had been introduced for the first time in 1916 and with it the right to object on the grounds of conscience. Seventy-five death sentences were passed in 1916 for disobedience, most on conscientious objectors who had been sent to the Western Front in the so-called Non-Combatant Corps. The deployment of these men on the Western Front was a cynical attempt to break their resistance. If it was hoped that by sentencing them to death they would abandon their objection the hope was misconceived. It was rightly thought that the execution of any of these men would undermine public support. There was less reluctance to consider public opinion in the cases of soldiers and while none of the conscientious objectors were executed, three soldiers charged with the same offence were.

1917: Passchendaele

For the British Army, the year 1917 was dominated by the autumn offensive in the Ypres salient culminating in the battle for the village of Passchendaele. For the French, 1917 was the year of Nivelle's failure and the consequent mutiny of large sections of the French Army. The British Army also felt the impact of the French mutiny: Haig was forced to extend his army's front to relieve the beleaguered French of some of their responsibilities. The Commander-in-Chief also took a tougher line with mutinies in the British Army.

Courts martial overseas convicted a total of 126 soldiers of mutiny in 1917, arising from ten actual incidents. A further fifty-one soldiers were convicted of the offence in Britain.[35] The officers on the courts martial appear to have adopted a lenient approach to the mutineers and only two of them were sentenced to death. The Commander-in-Chief adopted a harsher line and confirmed both sentences. This contrasted with what had occurred in 1916, when eleven soldiers had been sentenced to death, but only one execution had been carried out. Haig, it appears, was determined to prevent similar events occurring in the British Army. Therefore, the French mutiny had a direct affect on the policy followed by the British Commander-in-Chief.

Apart from the cases of mutiny, the sentencing of the courts appears to have remained consistent with the pattern in 1916. Desertion remained the major cause of a death sentence: a massive total of 760 deserters were sentenced to death in 1917, ninety of whom were executed. Condemnations for the offence of cowardice, however, were significantly fewer than in the previous year. Indeed, the forty-three death sentences passed for cowardice in 1917 was even less than the number in 1915 when fifty-one men were condemned for the offence. The reduction here, though, was more than compensated for by the massive increase in condemnations for desertion. Overall, in terms of the death sentence 1917 was not markedly different to 1916, albeit with a shift of emphasis. The proportion of confirmed death sentences was also comparable to that of 1916, thirteen per cent in 1916 and twelve per cent in 1917. The offence of sleeping on post continued its trend of attracting fewer death sentences – only forty-one in 1917. However, in contrast to previous years, two of these sentences were actually carried out. Privates Burton and Downing of the 6 Battalion South Lancashire Regiment became the first, and only, soldiers to be executed by the British Army for sleeping at their posts in the First World War.[36]

1917 was a particularly difficult year for the British Army, particularly on the Western Front. Limited successes at Arras and later Cambrai were effectively cancelled out by grave disappointment in the Ypres salient. The French failure also had an impact on the British forces, which assumed the main offensive role as a result. The loss of Russia as an ally was a major blow to the overall war effort. The entry of America into the war would not compensate for the loss of Russia until the American Army was able to take the field of battle in 1918. After the Bolshevik revolution in Russia there also remained a lurking fear amongst the British High Command that the army might be infiltrated by agents. Perhaps this fear was also a contributory factor in the tough approach taken with two mutineers in 1917: both were executed on the Western Front in October, a time when concerns about events in Russia were becoming heightened. The first, Corporal Jesse Short, 24 Northumberland Fusiliers (1 Tyneside Irish), was executed for his part in the serious disturbance at Etaples base.[37] The other execution was of an Egyptian labourer who had been part of a riot involving five hundred labourers in Marseilles.[38]

The very character of the British Army was also in a transitional stage during 1917. Conscripts had arrived on the battlefield for the first time. Initially, this appears to have made little difference to the sentencing policy of the courts martial: the army had always been slow to adapt. Historians often regard 1916 and 1917 as representing one particular phase of the war, both years dominated by the large setpiece offensives which failed to break the stalemate. Likewise, sentencing trends by courts martial in 1917 were closely similar to those in 1916.

1918: Retreat to victory

In 1918, there was a sharp decrease in the number of death sentences passed for military offences: 504 compared with well over 800 in each of the preceding two years. This decrease was then mirrored by the amount of sentences confirmed by the Commander-in-Chief: thirty-six soldiers were executed, or seven per cent of the number sentenced to death. The Commander-in-Chief had confirmed eleven per cent of death sentences in both 1916 and 1917. It was unlikely that these relatively large reductions at both field and command level were coincidental.

The death sentence was passed for the usual range of military offences with desertion, at 445, being the most prevalent. Other offences seem insignificant in number when compared to desertion: there were twenty cases of cowardice, sixteen death sentences for sleeping on post and another four for disobedience. Executions also dropped significantly. The Commander-in-Chief only confirmed thirty-six of the death sentences: thirty-five cases of desertion and one case of quitting a post.

The dramatic fall in the number of death sentences in 1918 has already been explained. The combined impact of conscription and greater understanding of shell-shock appears to have changed attitudes towards offenders in the army. Executions were carried out for just two similar types of offence: desertion and quitting a post. Was there also an increased tolerance at Commander-in-Chief level? It appears that there was; the percentage of confirmed death sentences for the offence of desertion also dropped. In 1914 and 1915 nineteen per cent of death sentences for desertion were carried out. In 1916, after Douglas Haig had replaced John French, the percentage fell to thirteen per cent and in 1917 it dropped again to twelve per cent. In 1918, the proportion of executions for desertion was only eight per cent of the total number of death sentences for that offence, by far the biggest reduction.

The changing experience of the army on and off the battlefield appears to have influenced attitudes towards the death penalty at both operational and command level. The army had slowly adapted to its role and to the differing demands placed on it from within and without. Some of this was manifested in the sentencing of the courts martial. The response of the Commander-in-Chief, the highest arbiter in legal matters, also showed signs of dramatic change.

Having examined death sentences in the context of time we must now turn our attention to geography and how the demands of a world war impacted on death sentences in the British Army.

Geographic perspectives

Although the Western Front was the main theatre of the war, other theatres should not be overlooked. Huge resources were directed to disparate parts of the world in an effort to bring a speedy conclusion to the war. Most of these efforts were directed against the Turkish Army. The nature of warfare in these other theatres occasionally resembled that of the Western Front – trenches and stalemate – but often very different demands were placed on the army. The war in Mesopotamia and Palestine, for example, was mainly one of movement. Conditions in these places were harsh: severe heat and disease continually took their toll. Unfortunately, not all of the statistics for what are termed 'non-battle casualties' (soldiers lost to illness or disease) are available but to avoid ambiguity all references to casualties in this section will specify battle, non-battle or all casualties.

Did the number and distribution of death sentences differ from one theatre of war to another? Death sentences passed on the Western Front were certainly greater in number, but we must also consider other differences between the various theatres of the war. Unfortunately, once again, incomplete records limit the possibilities of an accurate analysis: in the courts martial registers the theatre of the war has only occasionally been written in, most entries merely record the location as 'in the field'. An attempt to compensate for this has been made: the unit in which an individual was serving at the time of a death sentence can be located by cross-referring each case with E. A. James' study, *British Regiments, 1914-18*.[39] Apart from the sheer enormity of the task, this method has its own problems: a unit may have been moved between the time of the offence and the court martial and occasionally unit identification is impossible because the battalion number has not been recorded in the register. The location of some cases, therefore, is simply untraceable.

The British Army was of course an imperial army which drew widely on the resources of the Empire, in particular benefitting from a constant supply of soldiers from the Dominions and colonies. Later in this chapter we will examine the relationship between death sentences and the racial origins of different troops. A separate chapter deals with the Indian Army, which appears to have enjoyed a status all of its own. Other colonial units are also dealt with in the later chapter.

The Western Front

The Western Front was considered by many to be the most important theatre of the war and most of the British Army's resources were directed to operations in France and Flanders. This status was the subject of much debate amongst both generals and politicians. However, the 'easterners' lost out to the 'westerners' following the debacle at Gallipoli. The size of the British Expeditionary Force on the Western Front grew by staggering proportions over the four years of war: the strength of the British Army on the Western Front increased nine fold from 1914 to 1918. The number of casualties, both battle and non-battle, grew at a similar rate as the table indicates.

Figure 2: British army strength and casualties on the Western Front[43]

Year	Average strength[40]	Battle casualties[41]	Non-battle casualties[42]
1914	220,572	98,866	78,557
1915	662,263	313,027	579,738
1916	1,337,055	651,662	643,921
1917	1,968,879	750,249	1,042,266
1918	1,989,374	876,250	1,184,004

It was not so much stalemated trench warfare which differentiated the Western Front from most other theatres, but the large-scale of the offensives which attempted to break out of it. Epitomised by the Battles of the Somme and Third Ypres they absorbed huge resources of manpower. Another important factor was the relatively close proximity of the Western Front to home. This influenced discipline concerns and consequently the courts martial: it was not unusual for soldiers to desert and make their way home from France- some actually made it. Almost 2,000 death sentences can be traced to the Western Front, far more than any other theatre. This is not surprising as so many more troops served on that front than elsewhere. The number of executions there was also far higher. This, in itself, may not seem surprising, but significantly, the proportion of executions commensurate to the number of death penalties is far higher on the Western Front. The average proportion of executions in all the other theatres combined is five per cent. On the Western Front the proportion of executions is fifteen per cent. A condemned man was three times more likely to be executed on the Western Front than if he was serving in one of the eastern theatres of the war.

Capital courts martial on the Western Front were dominated by cases of desertion. Desertion accounted for approximately seventy per cent of the traceable death sentences passed on the Western Front – 1,345 cases-- and almost ninety per cent of the executions – 261 cases. This may be indicative of the nature of disciplinary concerns in France and Flanders. It is also an indication of the seriousness with which both courts martial and the Commander-in-Chief viewed this offence. For the reasons discussed above this was not typical of other theatres of the war.

Other offences were less frequent on the Western Front. There were 143 death sentences passed for the offence of cowardice, sixteen of which were executed. Fifty-two soldiers were sentenced to death for quitting their posts, six of whom were executed. A further 289 death sentences for sleeping on post were passed but none were confirmed by the Commander-in-Chief. Three of the thirty-four soldiers sentenced to death for disobedience were executed.[44]

Two other offences, although occuring less often, appear to have been particularly harshly dealt with by the Commander-in-Chief on the Western Front. Eleven cases of mutiny were referred, three of which were confirmed.[45] This is a far higher proportion of executions than any of the offences already mentioned and is symptomatic of the concerns of the High Command, who sought to prevent further mutinies by means of the strongest deterrent. Most of the death sentences (seven cases) were the result of the riot at the Blargies prison in France during 1916, with a further two each from 1917 and 1918.[46] Two of the executions were carried out in 1916 and the other in 1917. Casting away arms was also harshly dealt with by the Commander-in-Chief. Five death sentences were passed for this offence during the war, two were confirmed. Lance-Sergeant Joseph Stones of the Durham Light Infantry, a coal miner prior to enlisting, was sentenced to death on Christmas Eve 1916 and executed on 18 January 1917.[47] Significantly, the only other execution in the British Army for the offence of casting away arms during the First World War was passed on an African soldier in German East Africa.[48]

Death sentences in other theatres of the war
The Dardanelles campaign was intended to deliver a knockout blow against Turkey and provide assistance to the Russian war effort. After a preliminary naval bombardment, an expeditionary force landed at several points on the Gallipoli peninsula. Unfortunately for the allies, the bombardment had destroyed any element of surprise and the land forces gained little more than a toehold on the peninsula. The commanders, whose strategies appeared as myopic as that of their Western Front counterparts, did not exploit the limited successes.

In the event, the Dardanelles campaign lasted from April 1915 until the evacuation of the peninsula in January 1916. It was fought by an army with an average strength of 163,466 officers and men, mostly British but complimented by soldiers from the Dominions – notably Australians and New Zealanders – and India. 114,743 of these soldiers (approximately seventy per cent) became casualties of battle.[49] Almost 3l, 000 of these were killed, with a further 7, 221 missing. The fierce nature of the fighting at Gallipoli was manifested by the relatively low number of prisoners taken.[50]

There were ninety-seven death sentences passed which can be traced to the Dardanelles, or Gallipoli, campaign. More than half of these were for sleeping on post: fifty-eight cases. Fifteen death sentences were passed for the offence of cowardice; four for disobedience; nine for quitting a post and one for mutiny. The offence of desertion attracted only six death sentences: there simply was nowhere to desert to. Only three executions were carried out at Gallipoli, one each for offences of quitting post, desertion and disobedience. This may suggest a more lenient approach by the Commander-in-Chief, Sir Ian Hamilton, than by his counterpart on the Western Front: the proportion of confirmed death sentences at

Gallipoli was just three per cent. Field officers, who had to deal with the day to day problems of the front line were more concerned about soldiers falling asleep at their posts and continued to pass many death sentences for an offence for which there was no precedent of execution.

In October 1915 British forces, acting alongside those of their allies, carried out operations in Macedonia. The fighting was spasmodic, but in common with operations elsewhere, the military commitment not only continued but grew steadily. The Salonika Front tied down a progressively larger contingent of British forces, rising from 61,000 in 1915 to over 200,000 in 1917, many having been transferred from the Gallipoli operation. By 1918, the status of the front at Salonika was reduced in line with the military commitment, but still tied up 160,000 British Empire soldiers. In addition to the military operations, the expeditionary force was also assailed by disease, most notably malaria. By the end of operations the total of battle casualties was 23,787, with an additional 502,543 non-battle casualties, mostly resulting from disease.[51]

Traceable death sentences – and executions for that matter – at Salonika followed the familiar pattern, sixty-eight death sentences can be traced to Salonika and four executions were carried out. Most sentences of death were passed for sleeping on post (twenty-two cases) but there were no executions. Desertion, once again, proved to be the offence for which the confirmation of the Commander-in-Chief was most likely. The Commander-in-Chief had to consider twenty-one cases of desertion, three of which he confirmed. The only other execution for a military offence at Salonika was for one of the three cases of disobedience that attracted death sentences.

Operations against Turkey in Mesopotamia commenced in November 1914. Initially, the strategy was designed to protect British interests in the Middle East, but after the failure at Gallipoli Britain was committed to a long drawn out war against Turkey, most of which was fought out in the impossibly difficult climatic conditions of Mesopotamia. Once again, disease was to exact a heavy toll on the British force, composed mostly of Indian soldiers, and operations absorbed progressively more troops. In 1914 and 1915 the average size of the British military commitment to Mesopotamia was 32,000, but by 1916 it had grown to 165,000. It grew further to 307,000 in 1917 and to 412,000 in 1918. Approximately two thirds of these troops were Indian. Total battle casualties were 85,207, but non-battle casualties, including disease, were far higher at 820,418.[52]

The hardships endured by the British and Indian forces in Mesopotamia were extreme. Poor sanitary conditions, during the earlier phases of operations, were cited as a major factor, along with the extreme heat, in the spread of disease.[53] The open spaces of Mesopotamia resulted in a war of movement which brought with it problems in evacuating and treating the wounded. There was also a major military set-back with the surrender of the British garrison at Kut-al-Amara in April 1916. Over 14,000 British and Indian troops were captured by the Turks at Kut, 4,250 of whom died in captivity.

The number and type of death sentences passed in Mesopotamia do not reflect the true nature of the operational and discipline concerns of the army there: unfortunately, there are no records for Indian soldiers, the bulk of the force in Mesopotamia. Courts martial of British troops may or may not be representative of the force as a whole, but some important points do emerge from the analysis of the forty-six traceable death sentences passed in Mesopotamia. In common with the other eastern theatres of war, sleeping on post was the most prevalent of the offences to attract a death sentence, but in the case of Mesopotamia two sentences were actually carried out.[54] The two other executions in Mesopotamia were for desertion, again reflecting the seriousness with which the commander regarded this offence: only seven deserters had been sentenced to death by courts martial.

Egypt and Palestine was a military commitment from 1915, when 89,000 troops were engaged in operations there, until 1918 when that number had risen to over 385,000. Fifty-nine death sentences can be traced to this campaign. They are fairly evenly spread across the range of military offences: cowardice, with twelve cases being the highest, followed by sleeping on post, with ten. One case resulted in execution: a black soldier of the British West Indies Regiment was executed for striking a senior officer whose colour is unknown, although it is likely that he was white.

Fourteen death sentences can be traced to the expeditionary force in Italy in 1918. British and French forces had been despatched to reinforce the Italian Army after the rout at Caporetto in the previous year. The British contingent remained comparatively small and never exceeded 100,000 troops; 6,321 became casualties of battle.[55] Almost all of the death sentences that can be traced to Italy were for the offence of desertion (ten cases) but none resulted in execution. No death sentences were passed for sleeping on post in Italy, which may indicate that field officers on courts martial were less concerned with this offence in the later stages of the war. This was also true of the other theatres of the war, where a general trend indicating a reduction in death sentences for sleeping on post can be detected from 1916 onwards.

One factor, which differentiated the eastern theatres from the Western Front, was the relatively low proportion of executions to traceable death sentences. On the Western Front the proportion of executions was approximately fifteen per cent, contrasting with the other theatres of war where the proportion was much lower. The highest percentage of executions in these other theatres is in Mesopotamia, where nine per cent of death sentences were executed. This figure is itself questionable as no records of the larger Indian Army have survived. In the other theatres the rate was considerably lower: Gallipoli – three per cent: Salonika – six per cent: Egypt – two per cent: Italy – nil.

It may appear from this that the Commanders-in-Chief on the Western Front, Sir John French and Sir Douglas Haig, adopted a firmer approach to capital offences than the commanders of the other expeditionary forces. This would place the emphasis on the role of the individual. In the British Army it was certainly possible for individual commanders to influence policy, if not actually shape it. These commanders, however, were products of the same organisation and training, not to mention class and background and there is little to suggest that either French or Haig were atypical. An alternative explanation would be that the experience of the Western Front was different to the other theatres, and influenced the actions of the Commander-in-Chief. There is considerable support for this if we restrict our analysis to cases of desertion only. I have argued that the Commanders-in-Chief considered desertion to be the most serious offence. Only one was prepared to execute a soldier who fell asleep at his post, in spite of the large number of death sentences passed for this offence in every theatre of the war, except Italy. A comparison of the cases of desertion in isolation shows a much more consistent approach by all Commanders-in-Chief who, it appears, confirmed an average of twenty per cent of death sentences for desertion. At Gallipoli the proportion was seventeen per cent, fourteen per cent at Salonika, twenty-nine per cent in Mesopotamia and twenty per cent on the Western Front.

French and Haig appear to be harsher in confirming death sentences simply because they were presented with a far higher number of cases of desertion than the other commanders. Consequently, French and Haig condemned a larger proportion of men to death.

The identity of the British Army – regional perspectives
The British Army of the First World War was drawn from the entire British Empire. Consequently, references to the 'British' Army can be misleading. Memoirs by German soldiers, such as Ernst Jünger[56], confuse the issue even further by continually referring to 'English' soldiers when they really mean Canadian. Units recruited in the various countries of the British Isles were often organised into divisions of their own.[57] Territorial divisions were prefixed with specific regional titles such as East Lancashire (42 Division), Highland (51 Division) or South Midland (48 Division) and so on. New Army Divisions were prefixed with Scottish (9 and 15 Divisions), Irish (10 and 16 Divisions), Northern (11 and 17 Divisions), Eastern (12 and 18 Divisions), Western (13 and 19 Divisions), Light (14 and 20 Divisions), Ulster (36 Division)) and Welsh (38 Division). A Royal Naval Division was also added in September 1914 and was numbered 63 Division in 1916.

Dominion units were also organised into divisions, reflecting their geographic identity. The Canadian Expeditionary Force formed Canadian Divisions, which were organised into a Canadian Corps in September 1915. The Australians and New Zealanders were also formed into two corps, popularly known as I and II ANZAC; another corps constituted solely of Australians was formed in 1917. The Canadian and ANZAC troops were consistently the most effective soldiers in the British Army, playing major roles in the capture of Vimy Ridge and Passchendaele. The Australians were the first soldiers to breach the Siegfried line and in the Battle of Amiens in August 1918 – Ludendorff's 'Black Day' – it was the Canadian and Australian Divisions, on the flanks of the British attack, which did most damage to the Germans.

Death sentences were passed on soldiers from every country. Only soldiers in the Australian Imperial Force escaped execution. The Australians' immunity from execution does not appear to have reduced their fighting ability but this did not prevent courts martial from passing sentences of death on them. What then was the relationship between the demographic diversity of the British Army and the death sentence? To answer this we must first consider the component parts of the British Army. This can then be compared with the distribution of death sentences between those component parts. Fortunately, accurate figures for recruitment in the various parts of the British Empire are available from the War Office's own publication but it should be noted that these official figures were restricted to white troops only.[58] A synopsis of these figures is given in the table on the next page.

Figure 3: Army recruitment in the British Empire

Country	Total enlistments	Percentage of male population
England	4,006,158	24·02
Wales	272,924	21·52
Scotland	557,618	23·71
Ireland	134,202	6·14
Canada (inc Newfoundland)	464,391	13·48
Australia	331,814	13·43
New Zealand	112,223	19·35
South Africa	76,184	11·12

What this reveals is that the army was mostly recruited in England. In fact sixty-seven per cent of the army, as represented above, can be regarded as English; nine per cent was Scottish; five per cent Welsh; two per cent Irish; six per cent Australian; two per cent New Zealander; eight per cent Canadian and approximately one per cent was South African. These figures, which do not include native labour corps, provide us with a useful profile of the army.

By using this profile we can construct a model which shows the British Army in a geographic context. Then, the proportion of death sentences passed on troops from the different countries that made up the British Army must be identified, which can be shown in a similar model. This will facilitate a direct comparison between the figures for recruitment and death sentences and indicate whether troops from any particular country were more likely to be condemned to death than others.

Identifying soldiers with a particular country is a more complicated task. In some cases detailed personal information is available – enabling the soldier's origins to be readily identified – but in most cases the only clue to a soldier's origins is the unit in which he served. Therefore, it is crucial that the country in which each unit was recruited can be identified. In the case of the Dominion forces this is a simple task: each Dominion provided an expeditionary force which was identified as such. However, some other units such as the Royal Engineers and the Army Service Corps are more troublesome and these have been omitted from the statistics unless there is sufficient information to locate individual soldiers. This does not alter the statistics significantly because these units accounted for such a small number of death sentences: the aggregated death sentences for the Army Service Corps, Royal Engineers and Royal Army Medical Corps only amount to fifty-six out of a total for all troops of more than 3,000. The cavalry regiments, many of whom can be identified with a country, only account for a further twenty-four death sentences.

The overwhelming majority of death sentences were passed on infantrymen.

Fortunately, the infantry regiments can usually be identified with the county in which they recruit. That only leaves the Regiments of Guards, which were also identified by the country in which they were recruited: Scots, Irish and Welsh. For the purpose of this exercise the Grenadier and Coldstream Guards are taken to be of English origin. Other infantry regiments, which do not identify with a named county, still have traditional recruitment areas, such as the Royal Fusiliers, recruited in London. In this manner approximately ninety per cent of the death sentences can be placed in the context of country of origin.

For this to be of use in this comparative exercise, we must satisfy ourselves that the regiments were indeed representative of the county, or at least country, in which they were purportedly recruited. This is important, for after 1916 there was an attempt to alter the traditional regional identity of the regiments. This was intended to avoid a repetition of the devastating loss to local communities experienced after the Battle of the Somme.[59] The introduction of conscription provided an ideal opportunity to implement these changes. However, the actual impact on the regiments is not very noticeable and I would argue that the infantry regiments – with which we are primarily concerned – largely retained their traditional local identity.

This assertion can be tested in a number of ways. Firstly, James identifies the towns in which the New Army battalions were formed: these were usually within the traditional regimental catchment area.[60] This method, whilst providing a good general indication of the regimental identity, remains unsatisfactory: no account is taken of the topping up of battalions with fresh recruits – probably conscripts – to replace casualties. A more specifically individualised approach is required, but it is impossible to identify individual soldiers from the courts martial registers, which do not contain individual service numbers.

Regiments themselves can be examined to see how accurately they reflect their traditional character by referring to any of the eighty volumes of *Soldiers Died in the Great War*, produced by the War Office in 1920.[61] These volumes, organised into regiments, list each soldier killed and provide details of place of birth and the town of enlistment or, if different, the town of residence. Reference to these volumes shows that in most cases dead soldiers can be linked to the county of the regiment, although it is impossible to state this in percentage terms: such a task would be a lifetime's work. This methodology cannot be extended to officers who were not recruited on a local basis but we need not be concerned as only four officers were sentenced to death during the war.[62]

Finally, the cemetery registers produced by the Imperial War Graves Commission record details of some next of kin. This was usually a parent or wife and is therefore a fairly reliable indication of a soldier's origins. Using executed soldiers as a sample group it is possible to test further my argument that the regiment in which a soldier was serving is a reliable indication of his regional background. In 125 cases, the next of kin of executed soldiers supplied the War Graves Commission with details such as a parental address, and ninety-five of these were within the traditional recruitment area of the relevant regiment. This suggests that in seventy-six per cent of cases the executed soldier had a residential association with the county in whose regiment he was serving. Furthermore, only in four cases – or three per cent – was the next of kin's address at variance with the country where the regiment was formed. This can be adequately explained by migration:

the war graves registers were compiled several years after the end of the war.

Therefore, death sentences can be grouped into countries by reference to the regiment in which each soldier was serving, thus enabling us to compare this information with the numbers recruited. What this reveals is that there is a close relationship between the number of men recruited in each country and the number of death sentences passed on men serving in regiments from those countries. Most death sentences (sixty-three per cent) were passed on men serving with English regiments. This is remarkably similar to the proportion of men recruited in England. Similarities exist for the other countries: Scottish soldiers were the subject of eleven per cent of death sentences passed; five per cent were against Welsh soldiers; four per cent against Australians; one per cent against New Zealanders; eight per cent against Canadians and less than one per cent against South Africans. In all these cases the similarities between the proportion of death sentences and recruiting ratios is striking. In the case of Welsh and Canadian regiments there is parity between recruitment and death sentences. This is not surprising and is consistent with a random distribution of death sentences. This information has been reproduced in graphic form in the appendix.

However, there is one striking exception to this: Ireland. The proportion of death sentences passed on Irish soldiers is far in excess of the proportion recruited in Ireland. Variations between the two percentages for the other countries are slight, but the disparity in the case of the Irish regiments – from two to eight per cent – is massive. Given that all the other ratios are so close, some even equal, the Irish ratio is especially significant.

Recruitment in Ireland had been problematic and the numbers recruited there (134,202) were comparable to the number of men recruited in New Zealand (112,223).Yet the number of death sentences passed on men serving with Irish regiments was 239, approximately ten times as many as the twenty-three passed on soldiers in New Zealand units. Furthermore, the Irish can be compared with the Welsh. Wales provided roughly twice as many men to the army as the Irish: 272,924 were recruited in Wales. However, rather than there being approximately twice as many death sentences passed on soldiers in Welsh regiments the reverse is true: the ninety-one men in Welsh regiments sentenced to death is little more than a third of the Irish figure. In fact the number of condemnations against Irish soldiers cannot be compared favourably with any other soldiers in the British Army. What emerges from these comparisons is the inescapable fact that Irish soldiers were four times more likely to be sentenced to death by courts martial than were most other soldiers serving in the British Army. It is to the treatment of the Irish that we must now turn.

The Irish question

It is clear from the previous chapter that soldiers serving with Irish regiments were treated differently to other soldiers in the British Army. At this stage we cannot say that the courts martial treated Irish soldiers more harshly than others: there may have been some external factor – events outside the army – which explains the phenomenon. We must explore a number of external and internal explanations to enable us to answer the question: why was the number of death sentences passed on Irish soldiers disproportionately high?

One possible explanation would be that the recruitment figures for Ireland were distorted for some reason, whilst those for the other countries within the United Kingdom were not. This could occur if, for example, soldiers were recruited in one country and joined a regiment of another. This had certainly been the case in the early part of the nineteenth century, when it could be argued that the British Army was largely an Irish one: many nominally English regiments actually contained a majority of Irish soldiers.[1] The number of Irish soldiers recruited into the army dropped dramatically towards the end of the nineteenth century, however, and by 1913 the proportion of Irish soldiers in the British Army was only nine per cent.[2] Furthermore, after 1881 Irish recruits were increasingly concentrated in distinctly Irish infantry regiments.[3] The proportion of Irish soldiers in the British Army decreased further during the First World War, partly due no doubt to disillusionment over the Home Rule issue and the inability of the government to impose conscription on Ireland. Between 1914 and 1918 the British Army was transformed into a mainly English army.

Some of the many Irishmen living in England or Scotland may have joined Irish regiments, but if this did occur then its impact appears to have been relatively slight. Irishmen who enlisted in mainland Britain usually formed Irish battalions within local regiments in a manner similar to that of the Pals. For example, the Northumberland Fusiliers contained six Tyneside Irish battalions and the Liverpool Regiment could also boast an Irish battalion.[4] The London Irish Rifles, a pre-war territorial unit, was known as the 1/18 London Regiment. Eighteen soldiers serving with these Irish battalions were sentenced to death, but for our purposes they have been counted as serving with English regiments. Interestingly, however, four of these soldiers were executed, a very high ratio. Another Irishman serving with the Canadian Expeditionary Force – and therefore counted as Canadian for the purpose of this study – was also executed.[5] If, therefore, the total for recruitment of Irishmen is a conservative one then it is not more so than the total for death sentences and executions of Irish soldiers. It appears that Irishmen enlisted in the regiment recruiting in the area where they were living, whether that was London, Liverpool or in Canada. An Irishman who wished to enlist in a particular Irish regiment probably made his way to the regimental recruitment office in Ireland. Therefore, it is unlikely that the recruitment figures have been distorted to any significant extent.

In the 'rush to the colours' in 1914 and early 1915 there was no shortage of recruits in Ireland. So-called 'service' battalions of the New Army were raised all over Ireland. Sir Edward Carson, at the behest of Lord Kitchener, provided twelve fully equipped and uniformed battalions from the membership of the anti-Home Rule Ulster Volunteer Force. When John Redmond, leader of the Irish National Party, gave his support to the war effort thousands of Catholic Irishmen, many from the Irish Volunteers enlisted. The UVF volunteers were absorbed into Ulster-based regiments such as the Royal Irish Rifles, the Royal Irish Fusiliers and the Royal Inniskilling Fusiliers. Catholic Irishmen from the south of the country usually enlisted into their local regiments: the Royal Dublin Fusiliers, Leinster Regiment, Munster Regiment, Connaught Rangers and Royal Irish Regiment. A total of fifty-two battalions were raised in Ireland, twelve from Dublin, six from Belfast, seven from Omagh, five from County Armagh and so on.[6]

However, recruiting in Ireland effectively dried-up by the autumn of 1915 presenting the British government with a problem. A government report into recruiting in Ireland was completed in January 1916, three months before the Dublin rebellion. The report showed that on 9 October the total of Irish recruits was 126,462, but that the trend was most definitely downward.[7] Although the report did concede that this was an 'insular' figure only because no account had been taken of Irishmen enlisting on the British mainland, it was asserted that approximately 100,000 available men had not enlisted. The problem was most acute, it was claimed, amongst the agricultural population. The report remained optimistic in this regard adding:

The physical difficulties of making an impression on a scattered population of conservative tendencies still prevail, but signs are not wanting that the farming class are awakening to their responsibilities in this direction and the formation of farmers' battalions has come within the sphere of practical realization.[8]

Total 134,00?

The eventual total of 134,202 men recruited in Ireland over the duration of the war[9] (less than 8,000 more than had been achieved since October 1915) indicates that the optimism expressed in the report was misplaced. *Each Div, 12 ...*

Irish recruits might have been concentrated in the infantry more than soldiers from elsewhere but this is impossible to gauge precisely. Additionally, many Irish units were posted to Regular Army divisions where a stricter code of discipline was enforced than in, say, Territorial divisions. Most, however, in common with other British units, were formed into New Army divisions. An analysis of Irish units serving in regular divisions together with other British units suggests that within those divisions death sentences were more common in the Irish units than in English, Scottish or Welsh units. There were five Regular Army divisions containing Irish and non-Irish battalions: The Guards Division, 4 Division, 7 Division, 8 Division and 29 Division. Each division contained twelve infantry battalions and a pioneer battalion. In the Guards Division the highest number of death sentences passed on one battalion was the six passed on the 1 Irish Guards. Similarly, in the 8 Division the seventeen death sentences passed on the 1 Royal Irish Rifles is the highest in the division. The situation was not much better for Irish units in the other three divi-

Each Bn. Ave 7 death sentences 4 for

sions: Irish battalions received either the second or third highest number of death sentences. In short, Irish units in these divisions consistently came off worse than others. The overall average for English, Scottish or Welsh units in these divisions is four death sentences per battalion. However, the overall average for the Irish units in these divisions is seven per battalion. Clearly, this cannot be explained by reference to a differing disciplinary ethos between types of unit, for here we are directly comparing like with like. Furthermore, the difference is a substantial one.

There were other reasons which might explain the large proportion of death sentences passed on Irish soldiers. By 1914, Ireland was on the verge of civil war. Irish Home Rule became a live constitutional issue in the years before the outbreak of war in 1914 when the Liberal government became dependent on Irish Nationalist support in the Commons after the general election of 1910. In 1912, the Prime Minister, Asquith, introduced his Home Rule Bill to devolve power to a Dublin parliament. The Bill was to become law in September 1914, but the operation of the Act was suspended following the outbreak of war. Nevertheless, many Irishmen did enlist in the British Army and the Expeditionary Force, despatched to Belgium in 1914, contained two divisions from Ireland. The Home Rule issue had merely been postponed, although the dramatic events of April 1916 brought it very much to the attention of both the government and the army.

Opposition to Home Rule became militant and militarised among Unionists in the north of Ireland. When Asquith had introduced his Home Rule Bill in 1912 it caused great concern to many Protestants in Ulster who disliked the idea of being ruled by a Catholic dominated parliament in Dublin. Grassroots unionism responded by forming the UVF, committed to opposing any form of rule from Dublin by force. Yet at the outbreak of war, men of the UVF enlisted into the British Army, despite concerns that Home Rule might be imposed on Ulster in their absence, forming the backbone of the 36 'Ulster' Division.

By 1914 opposing paramilitary groups had been formed in the Protestant north and the Catholic south. Ironically, both sides had been armed with German arms: the UVF with 30,000 guns landed at Larne: the nationalist Irish Volunteers with 1,500 landed by Erskine Childers at Howth. Three years earlier James Craig, a leading Ulsterman and the first Prime Minister of Ulster after 1921, had hailed the Kaiser as a Protestant champion, a sentiment endorsed by another leading Ulster politician, Frederick Crawford, in 1912, This scandalised the Ulster Liberals who riposted with the pamphlet *The Kaiser's Ulster Friends*.[10] Remarkably, after 1914, Catholic and Protestant Irishmen lined up in the same order of battle. Both had previously demonstrated a willingness to oppose the British government to protect their own interests. Yet they had responded to their respective leaders' calls to enlist in the British Army: Catholics to Redmond and Protestants to Craig and Carson. Could the British Army rely on the unconditional loyalty of either Catholic or Protestant Irish soldiers?

The government was sufficiently concerned about possible unrest in Ireland to withhold two divisions from the BEF in 1914 to deal with any possible uprising.[11] The questionable state of Irish loyalty arguably provides us with the most plausible explanation of the large proportion for death sentences against Irish soldiers. This is a compelling argument that warrants further consideration.

Still

Despite the initial recruiting success, fewer men from Ireland enlisted in the

62

British Army during the First World War than from other parts of the British Isles. The proportion of the male population recruited in Ireland was little more than six per cent compared to an average of more than twenty-three per cent from the other parts of Britain.[12] Owing to political sensitivities, neither the Lord Derby Scheme nor conscription was ever imposed in Ireland as it had been in the rest of Britain after 1916. The combination of these two factors suggests that there was little lasting enthusiasm in Ireland for a 'British' war.

Paradoxically, it could be argued that these very factors amount to a confirmation of the loyalty of Irish soldiers. There may have been little support for the war in Ireland, but those Irishmen who did enlist in the British Army did so entirely of their own volition. They were not conscripted, nor would there have been much in the way of social pressure to enlist, which undoubtedly existed in the rest of Britain. Indeed, social pressure in many parts of Ireland would have been quite the opposite, requiring a great deal of determination on the part of an individual to enlist in the British Army. Irish soldiers in the British Army were therefore, an extremely self-selecting group whose loyalty cannot be seriously questioned. The analysis of political events in Ireland and of the involvement of Irish soldiers in the war supports this view.

The most dramatic expression of Irish discontent came in the form of an armed uprising in Easter 1916: armed Irish activists seized the General Post Office in Dublin and declared Ireland a Republic. The rebellion did not prove to be the catalyst for the immediate overthrow of British rule hoped for by its leaders and it was crushed in a matter of days. Nor was it evidence of Irish disloyalty. The rebellion was hardly greeted with enthusiasm on the streets of Dublin and, most importantly, Irish soldiers played a key role in its suppression. Two of the first units to be deployed against the uprising were the 3 Royal Irish Rifles, a reserve battalion from Belfast, and the 10 Royal Dublin Fusiliers, a service battalion formed in Dublin in 1915. Soldiers from Dublin and Belfast had remained loyal to the British commanders even when deployed against fellow Irishmen.

The rebellion did, though, cause concern among the British High Command and Irish units on the Western Front were initially withdrawn from the front line. However, the concern was not justified and the anticipated crisis passed without incident. A small-scale mutiny by Irish sailors in Russia amounted to very little and Roger Casement's attempt to form an Irish Brigade from Irish prisoners of war held in Germany, to fight against the British, ended in complete failure. Political events had tested Irish soldiers to the full but their loyalty had not weakened.

The battlefields also provided a test for the Irish regiments. In 1915, in a much celebrated incident at the Battle of Loos, the Royal Munsters made a heroic charge against the Germans. The following year, during the Battle of the Somme, the 36 Ulster Division fought with distinction at Thiepval, where they are now commemorated by the Ulster Tower memorial. In September 1916, during another phase of the Somme offensive the 16 Irish Division, containing men from the Dublin and Munster Fusiliers, distinguished themselves with the capture of the village of Ginchy. Irish regiments were bestowed with battle honours from all theatres of the war, and the gallantry of men serving with Irish units was recognised by the award of twenty-nine Victoria Crosses.[13] Among the recipients of the was at least one Irish nationalist.[14] There was no sign of a weakening of Irish loyalty in the trenches before or after the Easter Rising. British faith in the Irish however, was more fragile and the shock of the Easter Rising dealt it a near-mortal blow.

Superior race

British perceptions of the Irish during the first decades of the twentieth century were strongly influenced by nineteenth century ideas of race. These ideas placed peoples and nations in a hierarchical order. In Britain, the notion of a superior Anglo-Saxon race gained widespread support.[15] This assumed racial superiority provided an explanation as well as a justification for imperial expansion and the domination of supposedly inferior races. This justification for British rule was not only applied to India and Africa but also to Ireland. Both Blacks and Celts under British rule were thought by some to be inferior and incapable of self-government. Therefore, the rule of a superior race was deemed efficacious.

Query!

The idea that the Celtic race was in some manner inferior to the Saxon was common in English literature during the nineteenth and early twentieth centuries.[16] These ideas were often inculcated from an early age by their inclusion in children's books such as Charles Kingsley's *The Water Babies*.[17] Although first published in 1863, it remained popular and an edition with colour illustrations first appeared in 1915. Kingsley was particularly critical of Catholicism, a view that had brought him into conflict with Cardinal Newman. In *The Water Babies*, he created a fictional people, the 'Doasyoulikes', who were lazy and simian in appearance. He explained the cause of their predicament:

When people live on poor vegetables instead of roast beef and plum-pudding their jaws grow large, and their lips grow coarse, like the poor Paddies who eat potatoes.[18]

The stock distinction between English and Irish could hardly have been expressed more sharply.

Catholicism, which was closely associated with the Irish, was portrayed as another factor that differentiated the Irish from the English and much of the anti-Irish literature was in reality anti-Catholic in its tone. As Protestantism was an important feature of British nationalism, Catholicism was cast as foreign and incompatible with English-ness. Revolutionary activity in the Irish nationalist Fenian movement in the nineteenth century and the Home Rule issue served to heighten British concerns about the reliability and trustworthiness of Irish Catholics in particular. Catholicism, however, was not the sole cause of anti-Irish attitudes in Britain: there was a long tradition of purely anti-Irish feeling stretching back to the twelfth century, long before the Reformation.[19]

The arrival of Irish immigrants in overcrowded urban centres from the mid-nineteenth century onwards was a further cause of hostility. Irish migrants, according to Mary Hickman,'came into a society in which notions about the 'Irish' and about 'Catholics were already constituted as significant constructs of British national identity'. She concludes that 'anti-Catholicism and anti-Irishness were autonomously based but were concurrent and intersected'.[20] Traditional anti-Irish attitudes and later anti-Catholic beliefs were fused with nineteenth century ideas about race. The Irish were often considered foreign, inferior and unreliable.

Part of the appeal of racialist theory was that it could provide convenient answers to difficult questions. From the early months of the war the condition known as shell-shock troubled the High Command and the medical profession

64

alike. In Britain, the condition remained beyond the understanding of most psychiatrists and the use of psychological methods to treat nervous disorders was not particularly advanced.[21] An article in *The Times*, in April 1915, offered the explanation that the unconscious mind, itself the product of one's race, assumed control of an individual at moments of great stress such as those experienced during battle. It was this, it argued, which caused the soldier to break down.[22]

The belief that some races were more prone to conditions such as shell-shock persisted beyond the war. One witness giving evidence to the Southborough Committee of Enquiry into Shell-Shock questioned the soldiering abilities of certain races, including the Irish.[23] The committee, which reported in 1922, awkwardly concluded that, although shell-shock did not respect an individual's background (thereby explaining how so many officers suffered from the condition), the Irish, highly-strung artistic types and imaginative city dwellers were all more prone to it than others. One historian has said of the evidence heard by the committee: 'Every pre-war English prejudice was mobilized to explain away all those crack-ups at the front'.[24] Racial characteristics were cited as a predisposing cause together with 'education and social conditions and environments', in that order.[25]

Interestingly, a request from the Scottish Office, in 1920, to have a Scottish representative on the Southborough Committee was rejected on the grounds that 'the proposed enquiry will not follow the principles of nationality and if Scotland is represented, the medical profession and Ireland may claim a like privilege.'[26] The reason for resisting any possible Irish involvement probably had more to do with the poor state of Anglo-Irish relations at the time than with any anti-Irish conspiracy, but it indicates that the issue of race remained a sensitive one.

To what extent was the British Army influenced by anti-Irish social attitudes? Anti-Irish beliefs and anti-Irish literature was widespread. All levels of society were affected and there is no reason to assume the army was an exception. But it was the officer class, those who sat on the courts martial and decided the fate of those in their charge, whose ideas were most important. Senior and junior officers were usually products of the public schools, although this was diluted somewhat as casualties took a heavy toll of officers in particular. They were taught to value the Empire and the perpetuation of the British Empire was often justified by reference to supposed Anglo-Saxon racial superiority.[27] Inferior races included Indians, Africans and of course the Irish. Literature gave powerful expression to anti-Irish feeling and commissioned officers of the old and new armies (generally educated men) would have been exposed to such writings.

The Curragh Mutiny of March 1914 was an indication of how some senior officers in the British Army regarded the situation in Ireland before the war. Fifty-five of the seventy cavalry officers stationed at Curragh camp risked dismissal from the army in preference to being deployed against Protestants in Ulster. Alan Clark has argued that this amounted to little more than a protest by the army against being dragged into Irish politics and that it does not amount to evidence of the army choosing one side over another.[28] This view is wholly unsatisfactory. The refusal of the officers was expressly based on grounds of religion and it is tempting to ponder whether such a protest would have occurred had the deployment been against Catholic or Nationalist Irish. Some influential army officers were openly hostile to the idea of Irish Home Rule. One was Sir Henry Wilson, who commanded IV Corps during 1915–16 and was made Chief of the Imperial General Staff (CIGS) in 1918. He was assassinated by Irish nationalists in 1922. The CIGS during most of the war was Sir William Robertson. He had supported the Curragh incident and obstructed troop movements in Ireland to prevent any possibility of Home Rule by coercion.[29] The senior officer involved in the Curragh incident was Brigadier-General Hubert Gough, whose First World War commands included 7 Division and I Corps before being appointed commander of 5th Army in 1916. He later became Haig's main scapegoat for the British retreat in March 1918.

On the face of it, distinctions between northern and southern Ireland appear to have persisted in the British Army at the start of the war. In the New Army of Lord Kitchener two Irish Divisions were created (10 and 16). Prophetically, a separate Ulster Division (36) was also formed. The exigencies of the war itself however, served to blur the distinction between Catholic and Protestant Irish in the British Army. In his diary for 18 November 1915, Douglas Haig recorded discussing the issue of recruitment in Ireland with Redmond, the Irish Nationalist leader. Haig informed him of the problem of casualties and stated:

The Munsters are very weak, only about 500. He [Redmond] is to do his best recruiting them [Irishmen]. I have only three other battalions of Irishmen in this army [British 1 Army], viz., two battns of Irish Guards and the 1st Irish Rifles.[30]

Distinctions between Irish and Ulster units were dropped. Haig uses the generic term 'Irishmen' for all the battalions concerned without distinguishing between those recruited in the south, with whom Redmond might have had some influence, and those in the north, such as the Irish Rifles, with whom he would have had little.

Haig, a Presbyterian Scot, would have been aware of the sensitivities of traditional rivalries between groups with a history of enmity. On 12 January 1916, shortly after his appointment as Commander-in-Chief of the BEF, Haig recorded in his diary:

I passed the 6th Battn of the Cameronians – a Territorial Battalion which fought so well in May at Festubert. (The Regulars Battalion did splendidly at Neuve Chapelle.) It was proposed to put the 6th Battn (Territorials) into a Highland Brigade. The Battalion demurred and many said their grandfathers had fought against the Highlanders. So the Battn. is now under Divisional Hd. Qrs.[31]

The 6 Cameronians (Scottish Rifles) were a Lowland unit recruited in Hamilton. In this case, Haig had demonstrated that he was prepared to differentiate according to the background of a unit. The army, however, regarded the Irish units as Irish first and Catholic or Protestant second.

Several Irish units were deployed at the Battle of the Somme in 1916. The 36 (Ulster) Division contained six battalions of Royal Irish Rifles, four battalions of Royal Irish Fusiliers and three battalions of Royal Inniskilling Fusiliers: all Ulster units. By contrast the 16 (Irish) Division consisted of seven battalions from southern regiments augmented by five from Ulster. When the division was deployed once again at the Third Battle of Ypres in the autumn of 1917 its composition had not altered.

It appears that for the organisational purposes of the army, Irish soldiers were

Irish regardless of their origins. A division was a most important unit within the army. In previous chapters we discussed how the army was usually moved, fed, billeted and deployed by division. Senior commanders such as Haig constantly refer to the performance of divisions rather than individual battalions. The inclusion of Ulster units suggests that the Irish Division was denoted by its geographic rather than historical or religious identity. If religion had been considered an issue in the organisation of the army then it would have made more sense to augment the Irish Division with Highlanders rather than Ulstermen. In short, by mixing southern and northern Irish into a single division the army does not appear to have differentiated between Catholic and Protestant Irish. In the order of battle, the distinctions that existed between northern and southern Irish had been erased.

However, in the heat of battle and its aftermath, some differences appear to have been restored. During the German offensive in the spring of 1918, British troops fell back rapidly along almost the entire length of the front. Tens of thousands of British soldiers became prisoners of war in a single day. Haig noted in his diary for 21 March, the opening day of the offensive, that given the intensity of the attack the 'result of the day is highly creditable to the British troops'.[32] By the following day however, he had singled out one division in particular for criticism:

Our 16th (Irish) Division which was on the right of 7th Corps and lost Ronsoy village, is said to be not so full of fight as the others. In fact, *certain* Irish units did very badly and gave way immediately the enemy showed [my italics].[33]

Haig had ceased to regard the Irish Division as homogenous and attributed a greater degree of culpability to certain units within the division. Unfortunately for us, he does not identify which specific units these were. Haig's indictment of the Irish Division was both swift and uninformed. He needed an immediate scapegoat to explain the failure of the British Army to hold its position. He found that in the Irish, he had one that was not only convenient but also acceptable to politicians and soldiers alike. Haig was far from unique in this respect.

In truth, distinctions between Catholic and Protestant Irish were sufficiently blurred to render it impossible for anyone to identify units along religious lines. For example, the 2 Battalion Royal Irish Rifles, an Ulster regiment, was known to be ostensibly Catholic. Indeed, at the end of the nineteenth century many so-called Ulster regiments were said to be 'disproportionately Catholic Irish in the regular battalions.'[34] With the exception of the UVF inspired 36 (Ulster) Division, there is nothing to suggest that the religious inclinations of men in any Irish unit were apparent. To regard Ulster units as Protestant and those recruited in the south of Ireland as Catholic is a gross over-simplification. The assumption that Protestants did not live or enlist in the south of Ireland and that Catholics did not enlist in Ulster is clearly wrong. Trevor Wilson uses the example of a Catholic man from the south of Ireland who enlisted in an Ulster regiment to demonstrate that 'the enmities which divided Catholic and Protestant in Ireland were submerged by the shared misfortunes and expectations which brought men into this occupation [soldiering].'[35] This was also the case with the Tyneside Irish Brigade whose joint-founders, Felix Lavery and Johnstone Wallace, were a nationalist and a unionist respectively.[36]

Irish surnames might give an indication of a man's religion. Wilson's example, John Lucy, refers to 'the Macs and the O's, *and* the hardy Ulster boys' [my italics].[37]

Irish, like the Assures, reputed... undisciplined

But to identify a soldier's religion or origins merely by reference to his surname is not wholly reliable. For instance, not all the names of those involved in the Easter Rising are instantly recognisable as Irish nationalists or Catholics.[38]

Although the loyalty of Irish soldiers remained solid throughout the war, the perceptions of many British officers differed often regarding the Irish as perfidious. Once thought to be natural warriors, by 1914 the Irish, like the Australians, were reputated to be unruly and undisciplined.[39] Concerns about the Irish were often manifested in petty criticisms such as Haig's comment that the excellent turnout of the 16 (Irish) Division was all the more remarkable because it was 'a very difficult thing to get with Irishmen'.[40] The Easter Rising had magnified these concerns, undermining what little confidence in the Irish that had ever existed in the British Army. Irish exemption from the Military Service Acts magnified those concerns further still.

For many in the army a gulf had emerged between the British and the Irish who now appeared to be as far from British control as other 'foreigners'. According to John Bourne the initial resentment gave way to 'a more general feeling that the Irish were a 'bad lot' who had 'ratted' on the Empire in its hour of need'.[41] This did not represent a significant departure from pre-war British ideas about the Irish and little changed as a result. Haig persisted in his belief that firm British rule in Ireland would be salutary. On 30 March 1918 he wrote in his diary: 'The King said he was opposed [sic] to forcing conscription upon Ireland. I strongly pressed the contrary view not only in order to get men but for the good of Ireland.'[42] Other senior officers such as Gough did not agree with Haig, but their opposition to the imposition of conscription in Ireland was based on concerns over Irish loyalty.

Siegfried Sassoon summed up the attitudes of many British Army officers towards the Irish through a fictional character, Captain Barton in *Memoirs of an Infantry Officer* (1930):

'If you want my opinion,' he grumbled, 'I believe those damned Irish had a hand in Kitchener being drowned. I'd like to see that fatuous island of theirs sunk under the sea.' Barton had an irrational dislike of the Irish, and he always blamed anything on them if he could. He wouldn't even admit that Ireland was an agricultural country ['rural' recruits were preferred to 'urban' ones], and since the Easter rebellion in Dublin it wasn't safe to show him a bottle of Irish whisky.[43]

Perceptions of the Irish such as these were common before 1914 and persisted throughout the war. The Easter Rising may have had some short-term impact on attitudes but probably only reinforced pre-existing suspicions. The impact of Irish exemption from conscription was equally ephemeral: highlighting the separateness of Irish soldiers from the rest of the army. The Irish continued to be viewed as different and foreign. This was mainly on account of their Catholicism but was also based to a lesser extent on their Irishness. The latter was the element of commonality thought to be essential in binding an army division together and giving it an identity as say the 10 (Irish) Division. Yet underneath, there remained an unspoken current of anti-Catholicism. The fictitious Captain Barton epitomised British attitudes: perfidious Irish nationalists provided a convenient excuse for British failure, only most officers were unable to identify nationalists or Catholics. The Irish regiments were simply regarded as Irish without further distinction. When Haig referred to 'certain' Irish units who had not fought well in 1918, he was seeking an accept-

68

able excuse. There could be no excuse that was more acceptable to the British than the unreliability of the Irish.

[handwritten annotation: X 10% of death sentences went to Irish]
[handwritten annotation: Even tho they only 2% of army]

Out of a total of 2,912 traceable death sentences for military offences passed by British courts martial during the First World War, 221 were passed on Irish soldiers. Even though the Irish constituted only two-per cent of the British Army, they were the recipients of eight-per cent of all death sentences passed. Even within the same units, such as the five regular army divisions examined earlier, more death sentences were imposed on Irish soldiers. It is unlikely that the disparity between the proportion of Irish recruits and death sentences was caused by the actions of Irish soldiers themselves: Irish loyalty in the army had remained firm in spite of external political events. I have also argued that negative British attitudes towards the Irish were current before the war and were unaffected by political events during it. To sustain this argument we must be satisfied that there is no significant relationship between the number of death sentences passed on Irish soldiers and political developments in Ireland. So, to what extent did events such as the Easter Rising influence the sentencing of the courts martial? *[handwritten annotation: Even before Easter 1916 Rising]*

From the start of the war in August 1914 until the Easter Rising of 24 April 1916, British courts martial passed 881 death sentences. Eighty-eight, or ten per cent, of these were against Irish soldiers. The number of death sentences passed before April 1916 may be relatively small but it still appears to be consistent with statistics for the war as a whole. Disregarding cavalry, three men serving with Irish units were condemned by courts martial in 1914. The first, Drummer H. Barrett of the Leinster Regiment, was sentenced to death on 2 November 1914 for cowardice. His sentence was commuted to two years' hard labour.[44] The following month two men of the Royal Irish Fusiliers, Privates Murphy and Reavy, were sentenced to death for an offence committed against a local inhabitant. Details of the crime are not known but the men's sentences were reduced by the Commander-in-Chief to five years penal servitude.[45] This suggests that it was unlikely to have been one of the more serious crimes such as rape, which were often tried under this section of the Army Act. The comparatively low figures for 1914 mean that it would be difficult to sustain any conclusions drawn from them. It is still worth noting however, that this was the only year when the proportion of Irish death sentences (four per cent) even remotely resembled the proportion of Irish soldiers in the British Army. No executions resulted from the death sentences passed on Irish soldiers in 1914.

In percentage terms, Irish death sentences peaked in 1915. In that year, Irish units were deployed in a number of locations, most notably Gallipoli, Salonika and at the Battle of Loos on the Western Front. Fifty-nine men in Irish units were condemned by courts martial in 1915 – one tenth of the 591 condemnations in the whole army that year. Seven Irish soldiers had their capital sentences carried out. The proportion of Irish soldiers sentenced to death in 1915 was particularly high given their actual numbers. This cannot, however, be attributed to British discontent with the number of enlistments in Ireland: the recruiting problem in Ireland was only revealed at the end of 1915. Concerns about Irish nationalism did linger, however, and a large number of Irish troops found themselves posted to places further afield than France. *[handwritten annotations in right margin: 1915, 59 20, death, 7 exec.]*

The first executions of Irish soldiers were probably a result of the hardship of the first winter on the Western Front. Privates Albert Smythe and Thomas Cummings of

1 Irish Guards were tried for desertion on 19 January 1915. They were found guilty and sentenced to death. On 24 January the GOC I Corps recommended that the sentence should be carried out:

These two cases of desertion with intent to evade operations against the enemy are clearly proved. The charges as framed, however, do not actually specify that these two men were avoiding any particular important military service, but it was naturally within the judicial knowledge of the court that the battalion concerned was, during the greater portion of the absence, serving actively in the trenches against the enemy. These two cases are particularly heinous ones, and I hope that the extreme penalty which has been awarded by the court will be approved.[46]

Douglas Haig, GOC 1 Army agreed, simply adding, 'I concur and recommend that the two prisoners be shot.'[47] On 28 January the two privates, aged twenty-two and twenty-seven respectively, were executed. The Guards were considered the elite of the British infantry. It is interesting therefore, that during the war only five Guardsmen were executed; three of them were serving with the Irish Guards.[48]

Another soldier serving with an Irish unit was executed on the Western Front in the following month. Twenty-year-old Private Hope of 2 Leinster Regiment was shot for desertion because of the poor state of discipline in his brigade. On 23 February 1915, General Horace Smith-Dorrien commented:

The Brigade discipline is the second worse and the battn discipline is also the second worse in the army. The case is a very bad one and I recommend that the extreme penalty be carried out.[49]

On the same day Smith-Dorrien recommended another execution for a deserter from the West Yorkshire Regiment because the discipline in his battalion and brigade was 'the worst in the Division' [my italics] and because 'an example in the Division is very necessary.'[50] Both soldiers were executed on the same day. What is interesting about these two cases is that both men were serving in the same 6 Division and Smith-Dorrien obviously felt that two examples were justified.

One execution resulted from the ten death sentences passed on Irish soldiers at Gallipoli in 1915. Private Davis of the Royal Munster Fusiliers was executed for quitting his post. In his defence he claimed that he had done so to go to the latrine. The court found him guilty and on 22 June 1915 sentenced him to death. The file from Davis' court martial then appears to have by-passed the chain of command and been forwarded directly to the Commander-in-Chief, General Sir Ian Hamiliton, who confirmed the sentence on 29 June: no other recommendations or signature appear on the file. The entire review process had taken merely one week. Davis was shot three days later.[51] The absence of any recommendation by the officer commanding the defendant's unit was almost unprecedented: the only other case in which such this happened during the war involved a black African soldier.[52]

The highest actual number of Irish soldiers sentenced to death by courts martial in a single year occurred in 1916 when seventy-five men in Irish units were condemned. In percentage terms too, this was still a comparatively high number, which remained consistent with the high percentage from 1915. Seven of these sentences were executed: a confirmation rate of approximately ten per cent. 1916 was also the year of the Easter Rising. Is this evidence of a relationship between the death sentences passed on Irish soldiers and the Easter Rising of 1916?

70

Out of the seventy-five death sentences passed on Irish soldiers in 1916, twenty-six were passed before the Easter Rising, the remaining forty-nine afterwards. It was normal for more death sentences to be passed in the summer months and therefore this ratio is fairly typical. Operations in 1916 were dominated by the summer offensive in the Somme region and, as we have seen, courts martial tended to pass more death sentences before and during these big offensives to reinforce discipline. Irish soldiers were deployed during the Somme offensive and were subject to the tighter discipline that accompanied it. The greater number of death sentences passed following the Easter Rising cannot be regarded as evidence of a change in the attitude of the army or courts martial towards the Irish. The proportion of death sentences imposed on Irish soldiers in 1916, however, was disproportionately high given that there were 856 condemnations in the whole army: the Irish share, therefore, was roughly nine per cent. Furthermore, it is interesting that the number of Irish death sentences reached the highest number in the same year as the Easter Rising and one year earlier than the rest of the British Army. *1917 Conscv- ipts*

There were fewer condemnations of Irish soldiers in 1917: fifty-nine were sentenced to death, five of which were carried out. However, the reduction in the number of Irish death sentences in 1917 should be understood in the context of changes occurring within the British Army in that year. This also sheds further light *domin – ant* on the relatively high numbers of Irish soldiers sentenced to death in 1916. By 1917 the character of the British Army had altered: for the first time conscripts filled the ranks. This of course did not include the Irish, who remained volunteers only. This had a shrinking effect on the Irish contingent, which became a comparatively smaller component of the army. Detailed statistics are not available, but it is likely that the percentage of Irish soldiers in the army was highest in 1916: the Kitchener/Redmond/Carson volunteers would all be present, but later replacements could not be conscripted. In spite of the reduction in number, death sentences passed on Irish soldiers in 1917 remained disproportionately high (approximately seven per cent of the 904 total condemnations). The proportion of Irishmen in the army was probably well below two per cent by this stage, but still seven per cent of all death sentences were passed on Irish soldiers.

There was no alteration in this trend during 1918 when it is likely that the number of Irish soldiers was lower still. Twenty-eight out of a total of 515 death sentences were passed on Irish soldiers in 1918. The actual proportion, therefore, was roughly the same as it had been in 1917. Amongst the three Irish soldiers who had their sentences carried out was another man serving with the Irish Guards. Twenty-three year-old Private Benjamin O'Connell from Wexford in Ireland was sentenced to death on 5 July 1918 for desertion. He was shot two weeks later on 8 August 1918.[53] Around the same time another Irish soldier , Private J. Dowling of the Connaught Rangers was convicted of assisting the enemy whilst being a prisoner of war. The charge, brought under Section 4.5 of the Army Act, was a highly unusual one. Dowling had been captured by the Germans and had then joined Roger Casement's Irish Brigade. Unfortunately for him he was then recaptured and put on trial at the Guildhall in London where he was sentenced to death. Political sensitivities might have played a part in the final decision, especially in light of the tide of hostility aroused in Ireland by the Easter Rising executions in 1916, and Dowling had his sentence reduced to penal servitude for life.[54]

Minorities treated more harshly in Belgian + German armies

After the armistice some Irish troops, in common with other units, were retained on active service. During the period 1918–1920 the Irish had a harsh brush with British military justice. Events in Ireland, on this occasion, were at the root of discontent amongst Irish soldiers. Many men of the Connaught Rangers, posted to India, staged a mutiny in 1920 to protest about British atrocities in Ireland. Two of the mutinous men were killed as the mutiny was suppressed and sixty-nine were tried for their part in it. Thirteen of these were sentenced to death by the court. All had their sentences reduced to penal servitude for life, except twenty-year-old Private James Daly from County Westmeath who was executed on 2 November 1920. Two other Irish soldiers, Privates Flynn and Hardy of the Royal Dublin Fusiliers, were sentenced to death for murder in Turkey. Hardy, who was convicted of two murders, had his sentence reduced to penal servitude for life, but Flynn, who was convicted of a single crime, was executed in Constantinople on 6 November 1920. The number of death sentences recorded against Irish soldiers in this post-war period was exceptionally high given that there were only thirty-seven other condemnations in the British Army during this time. However, the high proportion was, on this occasion, a by-product of Irish discontent.

Interestingly, the courts martial do not appear to have differentiated between units recruited in the north or south of Ireland. The total number of Irish soldiers sentenced to death was equally divided between the southern Irish regiments and those from Ulster. This also applies to cases resulting in execution. The registers of the Imperial War Graves Commission contain next of kin details for eight executed Irish soldiers. Four are from the south of Ireland and four are from Ulster. Unfortunately, there is no indication of the religion of the men.

Minorities existed in all armies and many were subjected to harsher discipline than other soldiers. The Belgian Army was dominated by a French-speaking elite. Current research suggests that Flemish-speaking soldiers were more vulnerable when it came to executions than were French-speaking soldiers. Christoph Jahr has shown that soldiers conscripted into the German Army from Alsace-Lorraine, annexed from France in 1871, were treated with deep suspicion. These men were subjected to a harsher discipline, kept in the front line for longer periods and had their mail more heavily censored than other soldiers.[55] How exactly this affected courts martial is not yet clear.

The Irish were not explicitly singled out for execution by courts martial but the pervading British attitude towards the Irish was one of deep mistrust and suspicion. The increased likelihood of an Irish soldier being sentenced to death by courts martial was not the result of any response to events in Ireland during 1916. Rather it can be understood as a symptom of generally poor opinions of the Irish as a race. The British had ascribed certain traits to the Irish; one was that Irishmen needed firm, perhaps even harsh, handling. There is no evidence to suggest that there was a deliberate policy of sentencing Irishmen to death. Nor is there any evidence of individual anti-Irish prejudice in the trials themselves. Pre-existing British attitudes towards the Irish provide a more satisfactory explanation. The British had considered the Irish unreliable before 1914: a view that persisted throughout the war and was manifested in the number of death sentences passed on Irish soldiers. This is what the historian, James Joll, described as *The Unspoken Assumptions*[56]: the hidden motives and reasons which lie behind decisions, in this instance the courts martial. The assumptions made about Irish soldiers, because they are unspoken, are not obvious and never explicit in the records of trials. To uncover them we must look behind the evidence at the sort of ideas which shaped the attitudes of those making the decisions. Literature and the social and scientific beliefs both of the time and of the preceding century shaped the backdrop against which perceptions of the Irish were formed. It is in the context of a general antipathy towards the Irish that we must understand the high number of death sentences passed on them. Remarkably, this remained relatively unaffected by the Easter Rising, which merely confirmed the British in their pre-conceived ideas, concerns and fears about Irish reliability.

He seems to repeat too much and maybe assumes too much

The imperial crisis

For after Spring had bloomed in early Greece,
  And Summer blazed her glory out with Rome,
  An Autumn softly fell, a harvest home,
A slow grand age, and rich with all increase.
  But now, for us, wild winter, and the need
  Of sowings for new Spring, and blood for seed.
Wilfred Owen, 1914

It is nevertheless true, and the fact is a disturbing and disquieting one, that a very large proportion of the men who offer themselves for enlistment in the Army are found to be physically unfit for military service.
W. Taylor, Director-General, Army Medical Service (1903).

Their men aren't brutes enough: that's the trouble. They're a crowd of devitalized townsmen, and that's the truth of the matter. They're clerks, they're factory hands, they're students, they're civilised men. They can write, they can talk, they can make and do all sorts of things, but they're poor amateurs at war.
H. G. Wells – *The Land Ironclads* (1903).

At the turn of the century the British Empire was in crisis. The war in South Africa had revealed profound weaknesses in the ability of the British Army to police the Empire; public confidence was severely dented. What should have been a small-scale war, the type preferred by the British, had ended up as a lengthy conflict that tied up 250,000 British troops. Moreover, the British were forced to seek military assistance from the Dominions. In order to bring the Boers to heel the Commander-in-Chief, Lord Kitchener, had resorted to a scorched earth policy. Solutions and explanations were urgently sought; a period of introspection coupled with the search for external factors followed. Paradoxically, the internal and the external explanations were not held to be mutually exclusive by their adherents. These concerns, however, were to have a profound affect on attitudes in the army and implications for those convicted by courts martial.

The Boer War was the last conflict to engage the British Army before 1914. All of the leaders of the British Army in the First World War had experienced the South African conflict. Lord Kitchener, John French, Douglas Haig, Ian Hamilton and Hubert Gough, to name just a few, had all held commands in South Africa. According to Travers, officers above the level of battalion commander (i.e. the generals) had not fully assimilated the harder lessons of the war.[1] Nonetheless, some of the experiences of South Africa did influence military attitudes: officers became afraid of being 'Stellenbosched', or got rid of, a practice named after a town in South Africa, where incompetent officers were sent to keep them 'out of harm's way'.[2] The practice continued into the First World War, only the term had changed to 'degumming'.

The greatest impact of the Boer War, however, was not directly a military one. In Britain, concerns focused on the recruiting crisis. In 1899, the Inspector-General of Recruiting had reported that in Manchester three out of every five volunteers for the army had been rejected as physically unfit. The journalist, Arnold White, published the discovery in *The Weekly Sun* on 28 July 1900,[3] whereupon attention was directed at the British working class living in large cities such as Manchester. Nationally, the number of volunteers deemed unfit for service in the army was calculated to be between forty and sixty per cent.[4] In 1902, the Inspector-General added his voice to the concerns about the deterioration of the working masses, the main source of recruits for the army.[5] In a memorandum to Parliament of 1903 W. Taylor, the Director-General of the Army Medical Service, agreed that it was the urban populace which was of particular concern and hinted at the existence of 'worthless men' within British society when he posed the question:

But the want of physique, thus shown to exist with regard to a large section of the community, is not only serious from its military aspect, it is serious also from its civil standpoint, for if these men are unfit for military service, what are they good for?[6]

These men whose worth to society he questioned were, he argued, destined to:

marry girls as weak as themselves, and have children, some of whom go to swell the lists of infant mortality, some to join the criminal classes, while others grow up more weak and incompetent than their parents [with the result that] the rising generation of all below artisan class includes a vast number of men of a very low standard of health and physique.[7]

Since the census had shown that more than three-quarters of the population of England and Wales were residing in urban areas the implications were regarded as very grave indeed. Taylor provided army medical board statistics covering ten years to show that the rate of rejection on the grounds of poor physique was one in every three potential recruits. However, he acknowledged that the true extent of the problem was far greater, because recruiting sergeants were encouraged not to allow candidates to proceed to the medical examination if they were thought to be unfit. It was believed, therefore, that the numbers turned away from the army might have been twice as large as statistics suggest, resulting in an actual rejection rate comparable to that quoted by the Inspector-General of recruiting some four years earlier.[8] Chief concern focused on the urban poor who populated the slums.

The writer H. G. Wells observed that the nature of war was changing and that battles could be won not only by healthy, strong countryfolk but by the application of technology. In his story of a fictional war the victory of a country of tough, though backward, rural people over one populated by weak townsfolk appears inevitable. Yet the trenches are eventually breached by armoured vehicles called land ironclads – a fictional forerunner of the tank. The rules of war had altered and in a battle of 'manhood versus machinery' the 'smart degenerates' had won, leaving the narrator to muse that 'as long as their science keeps them going they will necessarily be ahead of open-country men'.[9] The victorious townsmen were, he noted, 'not altogether degraded below the level of a man'.[10] It is important then to appreciate that not all those who came from the city were thought to be degenerate and that the term 'city dweller' was usually reserved for those who resided in the poorest conditions and who were thought to be of least use to society.

Responses to the crisis can be placed roughly into two broad categories: environmental and hereditarian. In other words some believed the cause of the problem to be the poor environment in which potential recruits lived, characterised by bad housing, poor sanitation and malnutrition, others believed that the problem was congenital. Distinctions between the two, however, were often blurred and there was a considerable overlap. The government's approach remained largely an environmental one: reforms were introduced to improve the living conditions of the working class, as well as their education and their health. In his memorandum, the Director-General of the Army Medical Service, unequivocally supported this approach arguing that:

Were all classes of community able to provide their offsprings with ample food and air space, a healthy race would be produced, and the proper material to fill the ranks of the Army would probably soon be obtained.[11]

Some private initiatives also adopted an environmental approach. Schemes such as the Scouting Movement were developed to encourage young people into the healthy countryside, away from the polluted urban-centres where the 'City-Dweller' had become *the* example of degeneracy, with its 'twisted or misshapen' body.[12] Daniel Pick has argued the notion of 'the degeneration of the Londoner receded during the First World War when employment became more plentiful.'[13] This was true of society as a whole, but it did not recede in the army where the stereotype of the degenerate city-dweller formed by the Boer War crisis remained part of the collective mind-set during the First World War.

Adherents of the theory of degeneration as heredity asserted that the unfit were far more fertile, producing approximately twice as many children than so called normal families.[14] One solution was to apply the science of eugenics, encouraging the fittest members of society to reproduce rather than the unfit. Eugenics, meaning improved breeding, was not a new concept, but the concerns raised by the Boer War gave it a wider appeal as a solution to what appeared to be an immediate problem. Often associated with the ideas of Charles Darwin, it is in fact the antithesis of Darwinism and the theory of evolution because it accepts that an improvement in the race cannot be achieved by evolution alone. This point was succinctly made by Darwin's cousin, Francis Galton when he suggested that the so-called struggle for existence, vital to Darwinian theory, 'seems to me to spoil and not improve our breed'.[15] The evidence of this, eugenists argued, was to be found in the urban slums where man had not evolved but degenerated. Furthermore, degeneracy, it was argued, was not limited to a physical condition, but was also responsible for a mental decline which was termed 'feeble-mindedness'.[16] Criminal and anti-social behaviour was often explained in terms of inherited defects. Those who supported eugenics as a solution tended to see the poor working classes who resided in the cities as inferior stock compared to those who lived a supposedly healthier life in the countryside. Outdoor pursuits were encouraged to improve the health of the nation and other environmental initiatives were aimed at raising the living standards of the urban poor. However, some eugenists preferred measures aimed at preventing the proliferation of the degenerate. According to these adherents of what Geoffrey Searle has termed 'negative eugenics', the remedy was the 'sterilisation of the unfit', a phrase supposedly coined by Arnold White.[17] To them, the unfit were an infected limb to be severed from an otherwise healthy body before their number spread and sterilisation was proposed as a cure for a number of supposedly congenital conditions. Eugenic ideas found favour with some members of the medical profession, such as the Liverpool physician, Robert Reid Rentoul, who published his views in *Proposed Sterilisation of Certain Mental and Physical Degenerates (1903)*.[18]

Eugenics had many influential followers, especially among the professional middle classes, and was supported by politicians in all parties, yet there was resistance from the Roman Catholic Church, and importantly, the radical Liberal MP, Josiah Wedgwood. Though concerns about degeneracy were sufficiently widespread in Britain that, according to one historian, 'there can have been few towns of any size which did not hold a public meeting in the 1909–13 period, to protest at the Government's passivity in the face of the 'menace of the feeble-minded',[19] the leaders of the Eugenic Movement in Britain, unlike their American counterparts, carefully avoided the sterilisation issue, stating that it was neither practical nor desirable. According to Professor Lindsay, a spokesman for the movement, 'the public conscience would be shocked by it, and a promising movement would probably receive a rude check'.[20] The options for eugenists included advocating voluntary sterilisation, the prohibition of marriage to unfit women, genetic counselling and contraception.[21]

Two problems remained for the eugenists: namely how to enforce proposed measures on the unfit or degenerate and the more fundamental issue of identifying those to whom the measures should apply. The first was addressed by adopting a more widely acceptable, and practical solution; placing the unfit in custodial care segregated from members of the opposite sex;[22] the second proved more troublesome. Terms such as the unfit and degenerate were vague and open to different interpretations. As early as 1835 J. C. Prichard, in his *Treatise on Insanity*, had attempted to delineate those he described as 'weak in character', and who included those for whom 'the degree of intellectual weakness is just such as to render individuals scarcely competent to manage business, or to conduct themselves with propriety'.[23] Prichard argued that sufferers were:

Careless, slothful, filthy, lazy timorous. At the age of puberty, they display the effects of animal instinct in the most offensive gestures and habits. Some soon become subject to fits of capricious violence, to hysteric attacks, to nymphomania or satyriasis; others grow dejected, melancholy, and sink under a gradual decay of physical health.[24]

The language used to describe degeneracy changed little during the following eighty years and in 1903 Dr. Robert Reid Rentoul included the weak-minded in a list of degenerates he thought should be sterilised. Others included lepers, epileptics, cancer patients, idiots, imbeciles, cretins, prostitutes and sexual degenerates. Rentoul also included confirmed tramps, vagrants and criminals in his list, together with dull and weak-minded children.[25] Other interpretations and definitions were attempted, all remarkably similar, yet suitably vague, encompassing mainly those who represented a potential burden, normally financial, on the rest of society. The term, 'the feeble-minded', coined in 1876 by Sir Charles Trevelyan to describe those who were unfit but could not be considered complete imbeciles, entered the vocabulary of those who concerned themselves with the degeneracy issue. However, later in the nineteenth-century and certainly by the early twentieth-century, following the Boer War, the feeble-minded had come to be regarded more as a sub-species largely due to the work of the neurologist Dr. A. F. Tredgold. In 1910, he argued for the existence of a distinct mental defect termed 'amentia'.[26]

The classification of so-called degenerates, whether mental, physical or both remained difficult and contentious. In 1860 the Swedish physician Anders Adolf Retzius published a paper arguing that races could be identified by their differing skull shapes. Retzius suggested that the Germanic and Celtic peoples, who had a dolichocephalic (long) skull shape, were different to the Turks, Slavs and other East-Europeans who had brachicephalic (short) skulls.[27] Racialists had used the theories of Retzius to classify races and so justify the superiority of white-skinned North-Europeans. In Britain this meant Anglo-Saxons. Seeking a scientific basis to legitimise their views, some racialists took to measuring skulls and jawbones to show that so-called inferior races – in Britain this usually meant the Irish -could thus be identified. It might have been this that Sir Arthur Conan Doyle, himself of Irish-Catholic descent, later parodied in *The Lost World* (1912), with the following conversation between the altogether simian (but English) Professor Challenger and the athletic (but Irish) Malone:

'Round-headed,' he [Challenger] muttered. 'Brachycephalic, grey-eyed, black-haired, with suggestion of the negroid. Celtic, I presume?'
[Malone] 'I am an Irishman, sir.'
'Irish Irish?'
'Yes, sir.'[28]

Other methods were also applied in an attempt to show that degenerates as well as races were distinguishable. Francis Galton, who coined the term eugenics in 1880, sought to record in photography the 'inherent physiognomic features of criminality and race'.[29] This, he believed, would assist in categorising those who should be segregated.

In 1904, A Royal Commission of Enquiry into the Care and Control of the Feeble Minded was set up in the wake of the recruiting crisis of the Boer War. Its report, published in 1908, acknowledged that there were three ascending grades of degeneration: idiots, imbeciles and finally, the feeble minded, who could be distinguished from the other grades of degenerate by their capability of 'earning a living under favourable conditions'.[30] This last grade concerned the commissioners most: during a fact-finding visit to the United States, they had been informed by an American doctor that 'the nearer they [the feeble-minded] approach the normal the worse they are'.[31] The commission accepted the principle that feeble-mindedness was an inherited condition (Dr. Tredgold had informed the Commissioners that in his opinion 80 to 90 per cent of feeble-minded cases were congenital) and supported segregation as a remedial action.

Concerns remained, however, and in December 1910 the Home Secretary, Winston Churchill, who had been impressed by Dr. Tredgold's work, drew the Prime Minister's attention to the problem of the 'multiplication of the unfit' which constituted, he argued, 'a very terrible danger to the race'.[32] Churchill was an advocate of remedial action arguing that the feeble-minded should be 'segregated under proper conditions so that their curse died with them and was not transmitted to future generations'.[33] Churchill, however, remained cautious about the use of segregation of the unfit if it had to be enforced through detention. This, he informed the government in 1910, could be far too easily abused:

In framing such a Bill great care must be taken to make quite sure that no one would be detained except on medical grounds. ... Otherwise the power of detention on the grounds of weak-mindedness might be used as a political weapon to remove inconvenient persons.[34]

By 1912, the Government adopted the definition of feeble-mindedness proposed by the Royal Commission, and which included vagrants, drunkards, criminals and 'those who it was considered desirable, in the interests of the community, to deprive of the opportunity of procreating children'.[35]

Attempts to legislate for the segregation of the feeble-minded and the prohibition of marriage with a defective met with considerable hostility and had to be abandoned. The opposition to the Bill was led by Josiah Wedgwood. In 1912 he raised the banner of individual liberty, forcing the government into a rethink. By the time that the Mental Deficiency Act was passed in 1913 its measures had been diluted, though it still included powers to detain, and in certain cases to control procreation. Other legislation such as the Aliens Act of 1905 was aimed at controlling immigration, arguably to keep eastern European Jews out of London's East End.

Immigration was also held to contribute to the deterioration of the working class. Not only was concern expressed about the quality of immigrants, but also that British stock was somehow degraded by the presence of immigrants, in particular the Irish. According to Daniel Pick, 'where commentators spoke in alarmist terms of the state of affairs in England, Ireland was cast as a kind of infectious malady, afflicting the hitherto healthy English body'.[36] To many in Britain, the Irishman was the epitome of the degenerate. Irish and Jewish immigrants headed for the cities where the decay was said to be at its worst.

The impact of the recruiting crisis during the Boer War had focused concerns on the military fitness of the nation. Although these concerns were concentrated primarily on the physical fitness of recruits, the mental suitability of working class men was also poorly thought of: the physical and the mental degenerate were often held to be one and the same – both products of a tainted heredity and prevalent amongst the urban poor. These concerns remained sharply in focus during and after the First World War. In 1920, The War Office Committee of Enquiry into Shell-Shock, chaired by Lord Southborough, heard evidence from a number of witnesses including the Medical Officer, Captain J. C. Dunn. He recalled the Boer War stating that: 'the Jews weren't worth their salt.'[37] Clearly, in the opinion of at least one officer the link between the Boer War and the First World War was sufficiently strong that he felt that he could recall an idea of the former to help explain an issue of the latter.

Fears about British military fitness had not receded by 1914. On the contrary, soon after the war started it was obvious to many that Britain would have to reach deeper into the barrel than ever before. The preservation of the Empire depended on the fitness of the working class to fight an extended war against a highly professional German army. The measures that had been taken to improve the fitness of the working class had yet to make any difference. Far from receding, concerns about the fitness of the nation were actually heightened. A recent study concluded that the Boer War 'was a vital component in the thinking of many officers during the Edwardian period and helped fashion the doctrines with which the British Army went to war in 1914.'[38]

The Boer War had brought the army firmly into focus for eugenists. The army became the benchmark by which the fitness of society itself was judged. This trend was not confined to Britain. On the continent the belief that the fitness of the nation depended upon the performance of the army strengthened, gaining momentum after the Franco-Prussian war.[39] According to Daniel Pick, 'the military came to be viewed as the litmus paper of national performance, physique and morale.'[40]

Eugenics did have some influence in the army, with some seeing eugenics and the military as natural partners, such as Colonel C. H. Melville of the Royal Army Medical Corps, Professor of Hygiene at the Royal Army Medical College. Writing an article in *Eugenics Review*, three years before the war, he stated his view that military service was eugenically beneficial for the nation:

Historically, military service has held the highest place among occupations in the estimation of the community, and its representatives have been consequently both highly selected by the rigours of the occupation and well placed for choice as progenitors of the future. Something in the ancient mode of struggle, at any rate, was related to the activities of the mating season among the lower animals, which resulted in the evolution of masculine strength and courage and the high esteem placed upon these qualities. For the whole of the period preceding history, and for most historical epochs in the life of active and dominant races, the test of efficiency has been conflict between men. Manhood and honour were primarily matters of the battlefield. The heroes of all the epics which furnished dominant ideals for long periods, were those whose warlike glory gave them favour in the eyes of the noblest women.[41]

Melville acknowledged that, in Britain at least, it was the Boer War that had established the link between the fitness of society and the army. He also argued that there was a eugenic relationship between the two:

warfare has brought men to such level of virility as they have attained... the nation realises [at times of danger] that she expects to have citizens who, in case of need, are not only willing but able to fight for her. An awakening of this character came, as is well known, at the time of the Boer War. ... It may be that an occasional war is of service by reason of the fact that in time of danger the nation attends to the virility of its citizens. [42]

Ironically, when the war started in 1914, such eugenic ideas did not match the experiences of a modern war. Far from being eugenic, war was in reality dysgenic. After just one year of war the original British Expeditionary Force was gone in all but name. On 12 October 1915, shortly after the Battle of Loos, Second-Lieutenant Cyril Rawlins wrote to his mother, and opined 'it is hard to see how to kill all the best men of Europe is going to mend matters: all the degenerates, all the criminals are left.'[43]

As the rate of attrition, on the Western Front in particular, gathered momentum, the crisis deepened. The army could no longer afford to be particularly selective about who it recruited. Medical boards, which previously had rejected some unfit

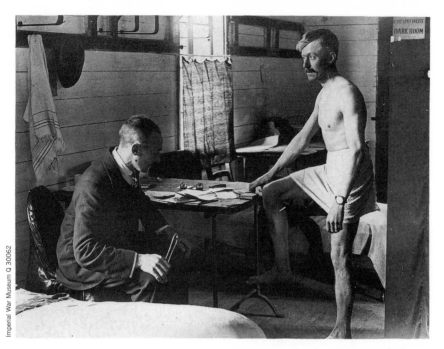

A medical examination: doctors were only paid for those they passed as fit for service

applicants, now found that they were expected to accept a more liberal interpretation of exactly who was fit to bear arms.[44] Britain's pre-war position as the only major European power to resist the move to a conscripted army was under enormous pressure. This had altered in practice with the introduction of Lord Derby's scheme, which finally became official when conscription became a reality in 1916. The army no longer comprised a select few. It had become an army of the masses, something which commanding officers were not comfortable with. The New Army did not arrive on the battlefields of France until the autumn of 1915. Acutely aware of the implications of a mass army, many commanders regarded the volunteers with deep suspicion. Travers has shown that at the opening of the Battle of the Somme in particular, where the New Army was effectively destroyed, the senior command was obsessed with discipline to the point of being more afraid of their own troops than of the enemy.[45]

Towards the end of the Battle of the Somme some commanders conceded that the New Army had done well. General Rawlinson, who had commanded the offensive, commented in October 1916, that the New Armies and Dominion troops 'have fought with a bravery and determination which one had never dared to hope for.'[46] Unfortunately, this realisation had arrived too late. The 'New Armies' had sustained such huge casualties that the offensive planned for the following year in Flanders would have to be fought mainly by the new conscripted army. The volunteers had probably been amongst the fittest young men in Britain, something never truly appreciated by many commanders. Their passing, so it seemed to many, meant that they would be followed by those who had not volunteered or by those who had previously been rejected by the medical boards as unfit for active service. However, the fitness of the early volunteers and by implication the relative unfitness of the volunteers and conscripts who followed them should not be overstated. Jay Winter has shown that from the beginning of the war regimental medical officers were inclined to pass virtually everyone who presented themselves for examination. Apart from any other considerations 'the examiners were paid one shilling for every man they passed, and nothing for every man they rejected'.[47] The result was that even in the early days of the war many who entered military service were wholly unsuitable. Indeed, when conscription was introduced the government attempted to rationalise the medical boards, with men being placed into one of three categories of fitness. This was later revised and potential recruits were placed into one of four grades. Nevertheless, amongst those soldiers executed by the British Army were some who, having been once rejected by the medical boards, were conscripted at a later time.

What the medical boards also had to assess was the mental character of recruits. This was an altogether more difficult task but once again there was little incentive for the examiner to enquire very deeply. Writing at the end of the Second World War Lord Moran posed the question 'can a board in a brief interview with a recruit recognise character?'[48] What all this meant was that commanders had in their charge men they believed were either physically or mentally unsuited to soldiering. Lord Moran expressed a view that those who lacked the character to be good soldiers should be weeded out either at the point of enlistment or during training otherwise:

If both fail to expose the latent weakness of the young soldier it is left to war itself to strip the mask from the man of straw, which it will do with a quite ruthless precision of its own.[49]

By the time of the Second World War this was by no means problematic: understanding of battle stress was greater and capital punishment was no longer an option for most military offences. During the First World War, however, circumstances were very much different. Men whose weakness was exposed in battle, however briefly, were liable to be shot. Men's character, like their physical condition, was widely thought to be the result of their heredity. Therefore those deemed degenerate in mind or body were held to be incurable. When concerns became heightened that good men were being killed tolerance of even the slightest sign of weakness was stretched to the limit.

It was not just the passing of the so-called fittest recruits that many at the time believed was dysgenic. A general feeling that the best and brightest young men were being killed pervaded the country. The deaths of talented, well-educated young professionals and artists such as Raymond Asquith (the Prime Minister's son and a barrister), his friend, the poet Rupert Brooke, and the composer, George Butterworth, all typified the 'Lost Generation'. Officers, many from the best families, most of them amongst the best-educated in Britain, suffered greater losses than the other ranks. Wilfred Owen lamented the passing of these elites with the sacrifice of 'half the seed of Europe' in his 1918 poem *The Parable of the Old Man and the Young.*[50] 'Blood and seed' had both become significant considerations of observers. The 'Lost Generation' of elites was no literary myth but a reality; war had indeed proved to be dysgenic.[51] Indeed, the realisation that war was dysgenic had an impact on the army very similar to that experienced in British society at the height of the degeneration debate immediately prior to the outbreak of war. Some military pundits sought to rid the army of those deemed weaker in body or mind in much the same manner as eugenists had proposed to remove the degenerate from society in general. Concerns in both instances focused on the infectious nature of the so-called degenerate.

The passing of death sentences and the execution of soldiers must be placed in this context. The commander of 22 Battalion, Canadian Expeditionary Force, Lieutenant-Colonel Thomas Tremblay was alarmed that after the Battle of the Somme, the massive casualties had been replaced by 'tramps and ne'er-do-wells recruited by other French-speaking CEF battalions'.[52] This, he believed, clearly represented a dilution of quality; his solution was to remove what he considered the cause. In an attempt to restore the character of his unit, he insisted on five executions and objected to the commutation of another fifteen death sentences. It is significant that his justification for such action was to draw attention to characteristics which would have identified the men as degenerates. In a war where the very best were being slaughtered in huge numbers, resentment had built up against those believed to be shirkers or degenerates. Interestingly, in the battle for the minds of their own people government propaganda often cast the enemy as degenerate: itself evidence of the seriousness of such an indictment. In 1915 no lesser person than Sigmund Freud lamented the way scientists had added their voice to this crude form of propaganda, complaining that anthropologists 'feel driven to declare [the enemy] inferior and degenerate' and psychiatrists to 'issue a diagnosis of his disease of mind or spirit'.[53] It is hardly surprising, therefore, that the army should also regard as degenerate those they felt had let down the rest of the army: those who could not or would not fight. Commanders often described these men as 'worthless'.

The worthless men

The number of men likely to desert in the face of the enemy is very small, and is composed of a few bad and weak characters...
Brigadier-General Lowther, 1st Guards Brigade, 1915.[1]

I have always pitied the coward, in whom battle arouses a series of hellish tortures, while the spirit of the brave man merely rises the higher to meet a chain of exciting experiences.
Ernst Jünger[2]

When an army is being trained to fight it must begin by weeding out those whose character or temperament makes them incapable of fighting.
Lord Moran[3]

In the years before and during the First World War the British Army was in a state of transition. In this respect it was not alone: the emergence of modern warfare had overtaken traditional strategic ideas. British commanders, unlike their continental counterparts, had no experience of mass armies – an integral part of modern warfare – and many had little faith in the quality of their troops. A lurking fear of being 'Stellenbosched' remained should an attack not go well and for the British Army during the First World War attack was considered paramount. At the Staff College generals, such as French and Haig, were taught that the bayonet rather than the machine-gun could carry battles. Travers describes it as the 'cult of the offensive', a Clausewitzian belief that superiority of morale, discipline and leadership won battles. Yet despite all the evidence suggesting that defence was the more effective strategy, the British High Command persisted in ordering offensives in the face of continual failure.

The commanders' lack of faith in their own troops also goes some way to explaining the obsession with attack. The offensive was considered to be easier to conduct because it actively engaged the troops, thereby reducing concerns about discipline. Within the officer corps there existed a 'suspicion of the reliability of working-class recruits'[4] This was particularly so in the case of the New Army formations which made up the bulk of the attacking force in the Battle of the Somme.

Evidence in the files of capital courts martial suggests that some commanders were prepared to take steps to eradicate the negative influence of the less able soldiers, those they considered degenerates, in order to reduce the influence on the rest of the army. In the minds of these commanders there was a whole army of men who were unfit for fighting because of heredity. Paradoxically, the removal of these soldiers was often recommended in order to prevent them from infecting the rest of the army. Some men were labelled as degenerate physically, others mentally. Some fell into both categories. A strong view existed amongst many commanders that whichever category a 'worthless' man fell into, his removal (i.e. execution) would benefit the army as a whole.

Shell-shock

The army's response to the condition known as shell-shock was one of confusion. The army was even reluctant to acknowledge its existence and medical officers never really came to terms with it. The traditional view, one held by most senior officers, was that sufferers were shirkers or cowards, suffering from funk. The remedy was often held to be extra duty to occupy the man's mind. But it was the cause of the condition that most confused the medical officers. Pre-war hereditarian explanations were found to be wholly unsatisfactory: as early as December 1914 a report to the Director General of the Army Medical Services showed that officers were more than twice as likely to be hospitalised because of nervous or mental breakdown than were men from the ranks.[5] Physical explanations were initially favoured, symptoms were often attributed to the shock waves of an exploding shell or even, in the absence of any explosion, the rush of wind caused by a shell passing overhead.[6] Shell-shock came to be defined in one of two ways: commotional shell-shock was caused by a *physical* action such as the force of an exploding shell whilst emotional shell-shock was caused by nervous breakdown due to the mental strain of battle. The nervous shock was never truly accepted as a genuine injury and even affected the allocation of pensions after the war, although that was also motivated by pecuniary concerns and provided a means of limiting the government's financial liability to former soldiers.[7]

Few British psychiatrists, let alone anyone in the army, were prepared to accept the use of psychological methods of treatment, which were disparagingly referred to as 'Teutonic Science'.[8] Early attempts to understand the condition fell back on older medical terms, such as hysteria, the association of this disorder with women only served to underline the belief that sufferers might have lost their manhood. In 1918, one senior officer offered 'unmanly qualities' as justification for an execution,[9] and in John Buchan's highly popular novel from 1916, *Greenmantle*, one of the heroes complained that fear 'seems to wash away all his manhood'.[10] Moreover, such characteristics were held to be un-British and associated with the Celtic races, a reason why the Irish in particular were also said to be incapable of self-government.[11]

The eugenist, Colonel Melville, had persistently referred to an association between 'manhood and honour' in *Eugenics and Military Service*.[12] In 1903, the Social Darwinist, Field-Marshal Lord Wolsely, had also linked 'virility of the race' with 'manliness', a view that was, in any event, commonly held in the military.[13] Effeminacy, by contrast, was associated with hysteria and with treachery. Defending an officer who had been accused of homosexuality, Raymond Asquith, referred to one of the witnesses as 'a fearful liar' and added:

He was not ill-looking but with an absurdly cushioned figure and a rather hysterical temperament more like a girl than a boy. He was the accomplice who turned King's evidence.[14]

It was also thought that over-imagination was a cause of fear. In Arthur Conan-Doyle's *Lost World* (1912), Malone (an Irishman) complains, 'I am too imaginative to be a really courageous man'.[15] Imagination like hysteria was associated with women.

Significantly, officers suffering from the condition known as shell-shock were usually diagnosed as neurasthenic, whilst those from the ranks were often diagnosed as hysterical. The psychologist, W. H. R. Rivers, who treated the poet Siegfried Sassoon, believed that officers suffered from a different form of breakdown because their education had instilled in them a sense of duty. This, Rivers argued, conflicted with the natural instinct to flee at moments of intense danger. The repression of this instinct of self-preservation, he argued, caused the officer to break down. Men from the ranks on the other hand, according to Rivers, were able to release this tension by employing 'sulphurous language which is one of the instruments by which the Tommy finds a safety valve for repressed emotion'.[16] Rivers' account, written after the war, demonstrates the influence of Freud's ideas about the unconscious mind, although Rivers rejected Freud's theory of repressed sexuality. Other psychologists, however, were attempting to explain shell-shock in Freudian terms at an early stage of the war. One such person was the psychoanalyst Dr. D. Forsyth who in 1915 wrote in *The Lancet*:

In every case, however, *the symptoms are directly referable to the strain of active service* [my italics]. But the various factors making up that strain are not of equal importance. Physical fatigue, hunger, and the hardships of trench warfare play their part no doubt. Rifle-fire, especially in the form of persistent sniping, is of greater consequence. But all these together are of less account than are the ghastly sights of carnage; these shake the self-control of all but the very strong, and when, as must often happen, a man sees his best friends killed or horribly mutilated the anguish of his own feelings may unnerve him beyond control, even though, curiously enough, the effect may not be felt for hours or even days after.[17]

By implication Forsyth rejects explanations of shell-shock based wholly on heredity. He continued:

But by far the intensest strain is shell-fire, especially by high explosives. The detonation, the flash, the heat of the explosion, the air-concussion, the upheaval of the ground, and the acrid, suffocating fumes combine in producing a violent assault on practically all the senses simultaneously, and the effect is often intensified by the shrieks and groans and the sight of the dead and injured. This mental shock is greatest in those who are most wrought at the moment of the explosion, and experience has shown that a high degree of nervous tension is commonest among men who have, perforce, to remain inactive while being shelled.[18]

For psychologists such as Forsyth the cause of the nervous casualties was the nature of modern warfare itself, in particular the constant use of high explosive and the inability on the part of the individual to help himself.

Yet hostility to new ideas such as these persisted, with many army neurologists rejecting the psychological approach in favour of traditional ideas such as 'tainted heredities'.[19] These explanations became less satisfactory, nonetheless, as cases of shell-shock increased, especially amongst officers, and it became apparent that 'young men of proven and respectable character were reduced to mental wrecks after a few months in the trenches'.[20] In desperation, the army appointed the psychologist Charles S. Myers as consultant to the BEF, in May 1916.[21] But the pervasive belief, even among medical officers, remained that 'if there was no signs of any *organic* disease then the patient must be faking it' [my italics].[22] Myers resigned his post in 1917, frustrated at the entrenched ideas and hostile attitude of the medical services.

The army, in the meantime, had not advanced in its understanding of the condition. Courts martial did show an increasing willingness to order medical examinations of condemned men, but few did any good. Medical officers consistently failed to allow for any inorganic causes in their examinations, which were often superficial rubber stamp affairs. There was a great fear that shell-shock was 'a highly infectious condition that was responsible for setting off mass panics'.[23] These disciplinary concerns fused with traditional ideas about degenerates which made the acceptance of shell-shock as a genuine condition very difficult. Pre-war ideas had linked degeneracy to a 'lack of moral fibre', a view communicated by a member of the Royal Commission in 1908.[24] The symptoms of the condition were also alarmingly similar to those associated with degeneracy. Dr. Forsyth identified two types of symptoms in shell-shock cases. He described these as 'nervous exhaustion' and 'neurotic temperament'. The former, he stated, was characterised by tiredness and depression. Sufferers were:

content to lie in bed, and want neither visitors nor books; their memory and concentration are bad; their hands are tremulous and they complain of dull headache and insomnia with hideous dreams.[25]

The more serious 'neurotic' patients also suffered headaches, insomnia and memory loss but they also:

Complain of local sensory or motor disturbances and are emotional or irritable, perhaps crying when they are spoken to or readily provoked to a show of temper.[26]

Patients, Forsyth argued, could also combine the two types. These descriptions are uncomfortably similar to the symptoms displayed by so called 'weak characters' in the early account by J. C. Prichard, which identified laziness, fits of violence, hysteria, dejection and melancholy as being indicative of 'defectives'.[27] Given that concerns about degeneration and the influence of eugenics was so widespread in Britain immediately before the war it is not surprising that symptoms, which today would be regarded as the result of shell-shock, were at the time interpreted as evidence of degeneracy.

There is evidence to support the view that shell-shock was associated with feeble-mindedness by some army medical officers. Private Hart of the Suffolk Regiment, sentenced to death in 1917 for desertion, had attempted to mitigate his sentence. He claimed to have been buried by an exploding mine and later passed as unfit for duty by a medical officer because of the state of his nerves. A further medical examination was carried out by Captain William Brown, 4th Army neurologist. His short report simply stated:

The above mentioned man [Hart] has been under observation in my ward during the past four days, and I can find no evidence of feeble mindedness or other mental defect in his case.[28]

Although the implication in this case was that such a finding might excuse the soldier's behaviour, such an outcome would have been the exception rather than the rule. However, it is the association of feeble-mindedness with shell-shock that is important. In the event, Private Hart was executed.

Identification and acceptance of shell-shock was one thing; treatment of the condition was entirely another matter. In an army and medical service where such conditions were viewed with deep suspicion it is hardly surprising that the treatment proved in many cases to be excessively harsh. For many it involved the use of electric shocks applied directly to the larynx to cure mutism, a common symptom. At the other end of the scale a talking cure was employed to enable the patient to come to terms with the conflict between duty and instinct. Rather than being mutually exclusive both types of treatment were often attempted by doctors who were increasingly prepared to experiment in their search for a cure.[29] This exposure to new ideas, combined with the increased use of psychological methods during the war, was largely responsible for a change in attitudes towards psychology in the 1920s.[30] Its effects on attitudes in the army are less obvious. The development of the abreactive, or cathartic, technique in 1917[31] might have improved the treatment of the condition, but does not account for the reduction in death sentences in 1918: it is doubtful that these ideas permeated either to the courts martial or to the medical officers to a large extent. Shell-shock continued to be seen as a matter for discipline rather than medicine: even Myers had suggested that shell-shock was 'an index of unit discipline'.[32] In this context it is not surprising that senior officers advocated either locking sufferers away in asylums or executing them.[33] Both were remedies of removal rather than treatment.

The confusion persisted after the war and this was reflected in the work of the War Office Committee of Enquiry into Shell-Shock, convened in 1919. Myers refused to give evidence, but evidence was heard from army medical officers such as Captain Dunn, who suggested that the soldierly qualities of certain races were suspect, particularly the Irish and the Jews.[34] Pre-war hereditarian explanations coupled with a persistent refusal not to accept psychology still dominated much of the evidence from senior army officers whose preferred remedy was greater discipline. One such witness, Lieutenant-Colonel Scott-Jackson, who had commanded a battalion of the Northumberland Fusiliers, told the enquiry that 'many cases of neurasthenia and shell-shock were 'skrim-shanking' of the worst kind'.[35] General Lord Moran affirmed that morale and discipline was the key but added that 'miners and agricultural labourers, and men *who lived open-air lives* [my italics], such as shepherds and gamekeepers were less liable to the disorder than the clerk or artisan'.[36] Others, however, were more influenced by the new approach. Lieutenant-Colonel Rogers, a Regimental Medical Officer, confessed:

I was inclined to look on men far too much as malingerers, and I very quickly changed my opinion. I think there is far more in psychology. I do not think malingering is common.[37]

However, Rogers added that hysterical conditions were not caused by shell-shock and that where they did occur the condition must have existed before. He did admit though that men were more likely to break down if exposed to danger for long periods of time, a notion expressed elsewhere with greater clarity by Ernst Jünger:

The notion that a soldier becomes hardier and bolder as war proceeds is mistaken. What he gains in the science and art of attacking his enemy he loses in strength of nerve. The only dam against this loss is a sense of honour so resolute that few attain to it. For this reason I consider that troops composed of boys of twenty, under experienced leadership, are the most formidable.[38]

The apparent contradiction between the belief that conditions such as hysteria were pre-existent and the belief that even the best soldiers were liable to break down if exposure to danger was common. This was due to problems in defining the condition as much as it was to any lack of understanding: each witness had his own interpretation of what amounted to shell-shock. For many it was restricted to physical injuries caused by an exploding shell. The complexity of the condition was recognised by the Medical Superintendent of the Maudsley Hospital, Dr. Mapother, who told the enquiry that cowardice and shell-shock were beyond the control of the individual, both being involuntary actions. 'I am not prepared to draw a distinction between cowardice and shell-shock', he said.[39] This, however, was exactly what courts martial were often expected to do.

Confusion was still apparent when the committee reported in 1922 and put forward recommendations to include training in psychotherapy for medical officers.[40] Whilst accepting that predisposing causes of shell-shock were both inherent and acquired the committee stated:

In the *large majority* of persons showing emotional shell-shock, there was present in the family history or in the personal history, evidence of weakness, instability or defect of the nervous system. Many feeble-minded persons, especially after conscription was resorted to, passed into the army. *Such feeble-minded persons were peculiarly susceptible to the incidence of emotional shell-shock and to the hysterical forms of it in particular* [my italics].[41]

Other predisposing causes cited included environmental factors such as education and social conditions. Significantly, the committee also noted the importance of 'racial characteristics'.[42] The American Army was also praised for 'weeding out' unfit soldiers before they were put into action. The British Army, however, sought to weed out those it considered unfit from the front line.

'Weeding out the unfit'

As the casualties rose so too did the concerns about the quality of the survivors. The army became increasingly alarmed that the best soldiers were being killed and that the shirkers and degenerates were all that would be left. Commanders were afraid that 'cowardly' behaviour was tacitly tolerated and sought out men to make examples of. These men fell roughly into two categories: those who were thought to be shirking their duty and those who were unfit for duty (degenerates). Often men were quite unfairly labelled.

In recommending the execution of a Scottish Private in February 1915 Brigadier-General Lowther of the 1 Guards Brigade said:

The number of men likely to desert in the face of the enemy is very small, and is composed of a few bad and weak characters, unaffected in their immediate fear, fatigue, or discomfort by thoughts of pay or gratuity. But if these few are able by their crime to obtain the safety and relative comfort of a prison their numbers would soon be swelled by others of only slightly less weak character.[43]

Being labelled a weak character was interpreted in a number of ways. It often meant cowardly, as in the case above, but it could also be applied to those who broke down under the strain of war. Either way, it was often used to justify a death penalty.

On 12 March 1915, Lance-Sergeant Walton of the Kings Royal Rifle Corps was sentenced to death for desertion. After his trial, a Chaplain, Reverend R. Hack, informed the man's brigade commander that he believed Sergeant Walton to be suffering some form of mental breakdown. Brigadier-General Oxley recorded on the court martial papers:

he [the Chaplain] tells me that, in his opinion, there are signs that L[ance] Sergeant Walton's mind is unhinged and that he seems incapable of grasping what has happened or his position; that there is a wild look about his eyes and he seems to forget things – he further states that the men on guard think that he is not right.[44]

The Brigadier probably did not realise that he was describing the symptoms of shell-shock. However, a medical report was ordered on 19 March 1915 asking for an interim report by the 22nd of that month. A certificate was completed on what is best described as a scrap of paper. The medical report, if it can be so called, stated that the defendant was 'of sound mind'. Seven people appended their unreadable signatures, the most senior apparently a Lieutenant, and French confirmed the sentence.[45] This had all taken just three days, indicating that the examination was merely superficial and intended, no doubt, to pacify the Chaplain. No observation was maintained on the unfortunate individual and, in all probability, the result was pre-determined. Lance-Sergeant Walton was shot on 23 March 1915, just four days after the report was first ordered.

Private Bellamy of the Kings Royal Rifle Corps defended himself at his trial on 2 July 1915. In his defence he claimed that he had twice been treated for a nervous debility, another term for shell-shock.[46] The court did not hear any medical evidence and despite the absence of any form of medical investigation the sentence was unhesitatingly recommended and confirmed. Private Bellamy was shot on 16 July 1915, for cowardice.

The case of Private Reid, Scots Guards, is interesting. In his defence he claimed that: 'I seemed to have lost my head'.[47] His immediate commander agreed and stated that not only was Reid of 'very good' character but that the state of discipline in his unit was 'excellent'. Unfortunately for Reid, he also stated that Reid was not a good fighting man. Although he recommended that the penalty should not be inflicted, this comment was seized upon by Haig as reason enough to ensure that Reid was shot, stating: 'I also note that the prisoner does not bear a good character as a fighting man'.[48] On this occasion the justification had shifted from the requirements of discipline to the individual soldier's ability.

This line of reasoning can be seen clearly in the cases of two Royal Field Artillery drivers who deserted together and were both sentenced to death by a court on 17 April 1915. Though the condemned men committed their offences jointly only one was executed while the other had his sentence commuted to five years penal servitude. The crucial comment came, on 19 April 1915, from Lieutenant-General Willcocks, the Corps commander:

Driver Bell is a determined shirker during a time of war and unworthy of being a soldier and an Englishman [my italics]. Driver Wilkinson might still be mercifully treated as at least he has since deserting done something to show he might alter his ways.[49]

The purge of unwanted soldiers continued unabated. In 1914, the nature of the offence strongly influenced the process of selection: the Commander-in-Chief had considered desertion far more serious than other offences (see Chapter 3). By 1915, the emphasis began to change. The type of offence became less important in determining the final outcome of individual cases – there were plenty of convicted deserters to choose from. The generals became more concerned with the individual's character and his future usefulness to the army. Consider these typical damning comments made by commanders in cases resulting in execution:

This man is worthless as a fighting soldier. General D. Haig, 1 Army, 28/5/15 (case of Hodgetts).[50]

The C. O. can know nothing in the man's favour from a fighting point of view. General D. Haig, 1 Army, 13/4/15 (case of Penn).[51]

Other criteria could also place a man into the 'worthless' category, once again reflecting another concern of the eugenists.

Private Docherty was in my own Company in Dublin, though not a particularly intelligent man, no complaint has ever been made as to his fighting qualities. Major E. S. Connell, 4/7/15.[52]

The man's intelligence, or lack of it, is surely irrelevant to a charge of desertion, unless it was used as a defence, which was not the case. Private Docherty had defended himself and claimed that he had suffered amnesia as a result of shellfire. Once again this soldier was executed. This suggests that other factors influenced the outcome of cases. Only rarely was the decision to commute or execute made solely on the circumstances or on the merits of the case. The man's character, as viewed by his commanders, or alternatively the state of discipline in his unit were far more significant in determining the final disposal of the case.

It was unlikely that the commander knew the defendant personally. His crucial assessment of the man's character was made on the basis of reputation and the opinions of other, more junior, officers. In an army where discipline was held in such high regard, a senior officer was not likely to risk his own reputation with the High Command by appearing to be lenient. This was a wholly unsatisfactory situation considering the weight afforded to his assessment. The probability of an incorrect, or prejudiced, recommendation was unacceptably high when balanced against what was actually at stake.

No allowance was made for the age, experience or marital status of convicted soldiers. Ages were not recorded on the court martial files and at least fifty-two executed soldiers were minors, two just seventeen-years-old and one of sixteen.[53] Few of these young men were represented at their trials. On one occasion in early 1915 a reviewing officer noted of the defendant, Private Briggs of the Border Regiment: 'His age *appears* to be about twenty-three [my italics].'[54] This shows that age was not of great concern to those who held the power of life or death.

In 1920, the Judge Advocate General's Office produced a report on thirty-two cases of minors who had been executed during the war. The report is a damning indictment of the military justice system. Of the thirty-two minors only three were legally represented by a 'prisoner's friend'. Seven were said to be of bad character, but three were apparently of good character. Previous convictions were recorded against only half of the young men, the other sixteen presumably had nothing against them. No fewer than ten produced evidence in their defence indicating that they may have been suffering from shell-shock. Alarmingly, the office also recorded that two of them were of low intellect.[55] This sample, produced by the army's own legal department, indicates that approximately one third of those executed could have been suffering from shell-shock, that legal representation was the exception rather than the rule, and that many men of good character and without any previous convictions were executed. One of these minors was Private Patrick Downey, of the Leinster Regiment, from Limerick in Ireland, who pleaded guilty to a charge of disobedience. No examination of the evidence was made at the trial. The young man was not represented. Nevertheless, the extreme penalty was inflicted on the twenty-year-old two days after Christmas Day 1915. Downey's crime: he refused to wear his cap.[56]

Prejudice frequently reared its head when senior officers came to make their decisive remarks. It was at this review stage of courts martial proceedings, that concerns about degeneration can actually be detected. Perhaps the most noteworthy comment was made about six so-called 'bantams' of the Durham Light Infantry. Bantams were soldiers who would not have been recruited in the pre-war period, or even at the beginning of the war, owing to their small stature. As the army required more men so the height limit was lowered enabling shorter men to volunteer for service. It goes without saying that these men must have had to overcome significant prejudice in their desire to serve their country. *The Daily Mirror* rather laconically commented in an article entitled 'A Chance For the Unfit', in July 1915, that whole battalions could be formed of men dying from consumption because they would, no doubt, prefer the hazards of warfare rather than '… a lingering and miserable death at home'.[57] Unfortunately, this type of prejudice continued at the frontline. According to Clive Hughes, 'the bantams were never entirely accepted' and the bantam divisions endured 'a spate of mostly contemptuous comment'.[58] The men concerned were all members of 35 Division, itself originally constituted entirely of bantam units.

A number of episodes clearly demonstrate the unsuitability of some generals for their commands. Take the instance of a night-time raid by the Germans on British trenches in the winter of 1916 when a considerable panic occurred and several members of the 19 Battalion, Durham Light Infantry (a bantam unit) fled to the rear of their own lines. An officer, Lieutenant Mundy, was mortally wounded and the Germans captured a private.[59] Night-time trench-raids were common on the Western Front, both sides conducting them regularly. The object was usually to harass the enemy, but more specifically to capture prisoners to assist in the intelligence and information gathering. To lose a soldier, as happened in this case, was bad for morale and also represented a successful raid by the enemy, which might explain why the incident was taken so seriously by the commanders. Six soldiers were charged with quitting their posts, two NCOs (both lance-corporals) and four privates. A further charge of 'shamefully casting away arms' was brought against Lance-Sergeant Stones, who had been in the company of the unfortunate Lieutenant Mundy.

At the trial, which took place on Christmas Eve 1916, the court heard from a military policemen that three of the defendants were apprehended without their rifles and that Lance-Sergeant Stones was in a poor state, hardly able to walk. Defending themselves, the defendants did not produce any medical evidence and relied on the court accepting their version of events, that they all heard an instruction, shouted in English, to retire. Needless to say, the court rejected this defence and all seven men were sentenced to death. As he was charged with a different offence, casting away arms, Lance-Sergeant Stones' file is separate from the file concerning the other six. Stones himself did not appreciate the significance of the prosecution's evidence that he was unable to walk, nevertheless the court ordered that he undergo a medical examination. The report from the medical officer simply stated that when examined (after the incident and presumably far away from the front line) Sergeant Stones was 'free from any *organic* disorder' [my italics].[60] The possibility of a nervous debility was not pursued beyond this.

It is on the file of the six charged with quitting their posts that evidence of the divisional commander's prejudice can be found. Firstly, though, the men's company commander commented on the file:

Their behaviour has always been good + as regards fighting they were good average soldiers doing what was required of them. They all came out with the battalion in Feb. 1916 + have performed their duties without any special distinction. L/C McDonald, L/C Goggins and Pte Ritchie have previously shown nervousness while under fire. Pte Ritchie was cast [i.e. medically retired] by the A.D.M.S. about a fortnight ago on account of his nerves. Dated 29/10/16.[61]

Remarks made by the brigade commander, Brigadier-General O'Donnell, on 1 January 1917 appear to confirm that, as suggested by the company commander, the six condemned men were no worse than most: 'From enquiries made the men in character and behaviour appear to be of the average in their battalion.'[62] The general continued:

The battalion, however, has not done well in the fighting line. They suffered somewhat severely from heavy shelling while in the Somme [underlining in red in the original document] fighting in July and were very shaky in the advanced trenches before Guillemont in August. I am reluctantly compelled to recommend that should the finding be confirmed the sentence be carried out, for the purpose of example and to show that cowardice in the presence of the enemy will not be tolerated in the British Army.[63]

In his remarks the general displayed a disturbing lack of understanding of the courts martial procedure and military law. He failed to appreciate that should the finding be confirmed then the sentences would be carried out regardless of his recommendations. He also made some contradictory remarks in an earlier part of his recommendation:

In each case the man has been found guilty of the charge and have [sic] been sentenced to 'Death'. I am doubtful, however, if the evidence is sufficient for a conviction.[64]

He had not understood the basic judicial rule that there can be no sentence without there first being a conviction. But it is interesting to note that he doubted the strength of the evidence which secured the conviction regardless of his comments.

Equally worrying, he failed to recognise that the battalion having been, in his own words, 'heavily shelled', may have been in a poor state of nerves. This would not only explain the 'shaky advance' in the following month but also might mitigate the offences with which the men have been charged.

The brigade commander stated that the soldiers were 'average in their battalion' but was clearly more concerned about the alleged poor performance of the unit. Despite his concerns about the evidence, he recommended that the death penalty be carried out on all six defendants. It appears that he had a low opinion of this bantam battalion, which obviously did not meet his requirements. It is incredible to think that Brigadier-General O'Donnell was prepared to sanction the execution of six men of 'average' ability against whom he believed there to be insufficient evidence. Some of these men were miners before the war, but a transfer to a tunnelling company had not been considered for them.

There may have been a hidden agenda. What the Brigadier-General appeared to be afraid to say, his divisional commander, Major-General Landon, who commanded the 35 Division, did not shy away from. His comments were dated 3 January 1917:

These 2 NCOs and 4 Privates have been found guilty of a most serious crime. They appear all equally culpable as soldiers, but the NCOs must be held as having especially failed in their duties, and responsibilities. There are, however, some 4000 men in the Division of whom 314 are in the Durham L.I. who are recommended for transfer as being unsuitable mentally and physically as Infantry Soldiers and it is probable that any of them would have behaved similarly under the circumstances described in the proceedings of this court martial. In view of the mental and physical degeneracy of these men I consider that though the sentence passed on all six is a proper one, the extreme penalty might be carried out in the case of the two NCOs and that the sentence on the four privates be commuted to a long term of penal servitude, and this I recommend.[65]

Not only did the Major-General share the low opinion of the unit, which is expressed by the brigade commander, but he recommends the executions also on the basis of the men's presumed degeneracy.

He went on to say that almost a third of his division was unsuitable and that they had been recommended for transfer. It may have been the Major-General himself who recommended the transfer of such a large proportion of his division, though it was probably as a direct result of a visit to the unit by the Corps Commander, Lieutenant-General Haldane. Openly expressing his unfavourable feelings about the men's lack of height at a parade of the bantams just a few days before the court martial, he had insisted that the names of the weakest looking individuals be taken so that they could be dismissed from the unit.[66] During December 1916 a total of twenty-six men of 19 (Bantam) Battalion Durham Light Infantry were sentenced to death by courts martial.[67] The official historian of 35 Division, H. M. Davson, conveniently omits this information from his account.[68]

On 18 January 1917 Lance-Corporals Goggins and McDonald, along with Lance-Sergeant Stones, all of 19 Battalion Durham Light Infantry were shot by firing squad. The four privates, in accordance with Major-General Landon's recommendations, had their death sentences commuted to fifteen years penal servitude.[69] The executions moved an eyewitness to write down his experience. This account was included in the pamphlet published by the Labour MP, Ernest

Thurtle. The anonymous witness described how he, as a military prisoner, had to collect the executed men's belongings and helped to bury the bodies:

I collected all the blood-soaked straw and burnt it. Acting upon instructions I took all their belongings from the dead men's tunics (discarded before being shot). A few letters, a pipe, some fags, a photo. I could tell you of the silence of the military police after reading one letter from a little girl to 'Dear Daddy', of the blood-stained snow that horrified the French peasants.[70]

This case highlights the methods by which a commander could purge unwanted soldiers. It is an example of the 'old' army rejecting the 'new' one: degeneracy is used, not only as the justification, but also as the criterion to identify a poor soldier. The small stature of the bantams made them an obvious target. Fifty-two sentences of death can be traced to soldiers serving in bantam units during the war, eight of which ended in execution.

In another case, Private Thomas Hopkins of the Lancashire Fusiliers could hardly be described as a model soldier, but his commanders, in reviewing his death sentence for the offence of leaving his post, went to extraordinary lengths to establish his presumed degeneracy. Hopkins, from Birkenhead in Cheshire, was a petty criminal who had been in and out of prison for minor offences before enlisting in the army. He had many convictions for vagrancy. In short, Hopkins fulfilled all the criteria that would label him as degenerate. He was admitted to the Mental Division of No. 8 Stationary Hospital on 22 December 1917 for the purpose of establishing his mental state. In the meantime the officer commanding the hospital took the unprecedented step of contacting the Chief Constable of the Birkenhead Borough Police. The Chief Constable's reply, dated 14 January 1918, was damning:

I beg to inform you, in reply to your letter of 9th instant that Hopkins in civil life was a boiler-scaler and so far as can be ascertained there is no insanity in his family, but in May 1910 the Medical Officer of HM Prison, Knutsford, reported that he was mentally deficient and it is believed that he improved mentally prior to his enlistment in the Army. I enclose herewith record of previous convictions and his general character in civil life was bad.[71]

The sheet of previous convictions showed that Hopkins had been sent to prison on eight occasions between 1909 and 1915 on various charges of petty theft and damage. He had thirty-two summary convictions for drunkenness, vagrancy, and assaults on police, though these were minor assaults such as pushing an officer or some other act that did not cause injury. The convictions recorded against Hopkins were all of a petty nature.

The medical officer's letter to the Chief Constable no longer exists on the file, but it appears that the Chief Constable was asked if he was aware of any insanity in Hopkins' family. If this was the case then it may be that the medical officer was investigating a possible hereditary degeneracy. The final report by Captain Montgomery of the Medical Corps, who was in charge of Hopkins' case at the military mental hospital, was obviously influenced by the Chief Constable's reply. He refered to Hopkins' convictions, his civilian occupation and the absence of a family history of insanity, reflecting the comments from the Chief Constable. He commented that Hopkins did not speak to others and it was difficult to get him to answer questions, adding: 'Patient is below the average in intelligence and is a criminal degenerate.'[72] However, he went on to declare:

In my opinion patient is responsible for his actions. He knew that he was doing wrong when he went away from the trenches his object being to avoid military service.[73]

Captain Montgomery's remarks effectively condemned Hopkins to death. The divisional commander, Major-General Deverell, commented: 'The prisoner appears to be a worthless man.'[74] The commander of 1 Army forwarded the papers to Douglas Haig on 30 January 1918 with the observation:

The man has a very bad character both in civil life and in the army. He is *probably useless* as a soldier. I am quite aware that the general *worthlessness* of the man is inclined to *influence* a [unreadable word] decision [my italics].[75]

The general's remark pointed to the likely influence of Hopkins' supposed degeneracy on the final decision and the soldier was executed on 13 February 1918.

Lengthy enquiries such as these were unusual and appear to have been reserved for cases where degeneracy was suspected. Generally, no enquiry was made concerning the background of soldiers before their fate was decided. Personal circumstances were not taken into consideration and in many cases an execution meant that widows, children or elderly parents were left with no means of support. One such case was that of Private William Nelson of the Durham Light Infantry who had volunteered for Kitchener's army at the age of seventeen. Whilst he was away in France his mother had died and his father was captured by the Germans. This was undoubtedly on his mind when he committed his fatal offence. He was sentenced to death by court martial on 1 August 1916 for desertion. The sentence was carried out just ten days later.[76] He left behind an eight year-old brother and a twelve year-old sister.[77] The army was prepared to spend a considerable amount of time and effort to confirm that Hopkins had been a vagrant, but no enquiry was made into the domestic circumstances of a man like Nelson.

Vagrancy, a major concern for eugenists before the war, might have been an issue in another case. Rifleman Albert Parker, from Watford, had joined the King's Royal Rifle Corps on 22 August 1914 as a Kitchener volunteer but on 4 May 1916 he was tried for desertion. Apparently, thirty-five-year-old Parker was discovered asleep and drunk after the rest of his unit had moved forward to trenches near Arras. Parker, who was not represented at his trial, claimed that he had accidentally missed the parade, but the court rejected his defence. He had a poor disciplinary record, with twelve previous convictions, including being absent. However, most of them were of a petty nature and involved personal hygiene: it appears that Parker was in a continual state of lousiness and refused to wash himself. Predictably, he was sentenced to death. General Allenby recommended that the sentence be carried out. The Commander-in-Chief, Sir Douglas Haig, agreed and just eleven days later Parker was paraded with his comrades and he was told he was to be shot without delay.[78] He was ordered to take off his cap and take one pace forward. According to Ernest Thurtle, a witness later recalled how he did so 'without a quiver', adding that 'a braver man at that moment wasn't to be found in France'. Parker was marched away and a few minutes later was shot by a firing squad made up of his own comrades. The strain was said to be so awful that at least one of the soldiers who had been ordered to witness the execution fainted.[79]

Another soldier apparently executed on grounds of his supposed poor character was Rifleman James Crozier, who came from Belfast. He had joined the Royal Irish Rifles in September 1914. Instrumental in his joining up was an unrelated Major Frank Crozier, who had promised the young man's mother that he would personally look after her son.[80] After being sentenced to death for desertion the young Crozier's case was referred to his battalion commander, the same Frank Crozier, by this time a Lieutenant-Colonel. His remarks, on 15 February 1916, were both typical and damning: 'from a fighting point of view this soldier is of no value. His behaviour has been that of a shirker for the past three months.'[81] The eighteen-year-old rifleman was shot at dawn on 27 February 1916. The brigade commander's comments reflected the attitude of the 'old army' commanders towards the men of the 'new', Kitchener battalions: 'the discipline of the 9th R.I. Rifles is good for a service [i.e. New Army] battalion.'[82] Clearly, this Brigadier-General at least, regarded the volunteer units as undisciplined.

A Jewish soldier from the East End of London, Private Abraham Beverstein, who served under the name of Harris, was executed in March 1916. Once again, here was a case of a man whose nerves had broken and whose commanders regarded him as being of no further use. Beverstein defended himself at his trial and stated to the court: 'I left the trenches because three rifle grenades exploded near me and I was deafened and my nerves had gone a bit. I felt nervous and lost my head.'[83] As has already been argued such a defence was probably more likely to bring about a sentence of death than it was to gain the sympathy of either the court or of the reviewing officers. This is what happened, despite Second-Lieutenant Redford stating that Beverstein was not only of good character but had been keen to come out to the Western Front with his battalion. Unfortunately, the comments of the reviewing officers are not attached to the file.

Questions were asked in Parliament about another executed soldier described as 'mentally weak.'[84] It is unclear how the court had interpreted this expression and whether the soldier was low in intellect or unstable. The soldier concerned was Private Ernest Horler of the West Yorkshire Regiment. During his military service he had frequently reported sick with what appeared to be trivial and unsubstantiated complaints. This might have labelled him as unfit in the eyes of the court. Furthermore, his conduct at his trial suggests that he was of low intelligence. At his court martial, Horler, stated to the panel:

I have been ill. I have been deprived of pay and am sure there is a lot due to me. I should like to apply for a medical board on my physical and mental condition.[85]

Assuming that they were untrue, the claims about pay, along with Horler's medical complaints, suggest that he was emotionally disturbed, but at no stage did anyone, either at the court martial or afterwards, question the fact that this man was not legally represented. Despite this, there was obviously a doubt as to his mental capacity and the court ordered a report on his condition.

The medical officer's report, dated 1 February 1918, stated that Horler had reported sick on five occasions and that each complaint was not only trivial but also unsubstantiated. This may have suggested that Horler was a malingerer and his divisional commander wasted no time in recommending that he be shot. On the same day that the medical officer had reported, Major-General Deverell simply stated 'the prisoner appears to be a worthless man'.[86] In an undated memorandum from General Haldane, Horler was said to have complained of 'heart bad, arteries poisoned by an injection. Stomach also poisoned'.[87] Despite acknowledging the good state of discipline in the unit, General Haldane recommended death on the grounds that Horler was a 'worthless man'.[88] This all too familiar term was tantamount to signing the unfortunate individual's death warrant and Horler was executed on 17 February 1918.

A soldier in an Irish regiment was executed after being described as the 'worst character in the army'. Private Hendricks, 2 Battalion Leinster Regiment, had claimed at his trial that he was an American citizen and also that he had served in the Boer War. Unfortunately, it has not been possible to verify this. Once again, discipline in the battalion was said to be good but on 27 July 1918, the Brigade Commander commented:

This man is one of the worst characters in the army, he openly defies authority and deliberately commits crime. He is the worst influence in his Regiment and is valueless as a soldier.[89]

Hendricks was also said to be an accomplished escaper but there is nothing to support this on the file. He was not charged with escaping from custody and the only indication on his service record that he may ever have done so is a previous conviction for 'negligently losing a pair of army handcuffs'.[90]

If further evidence is required of a 'weeding out' process then one needs to look no further than the cases of the only two officers who were executed for military offences during the war.[91] In both there was a long history of diagnosed nervous disorder and it can be said, with some confidence, that these two shell-shocked officers were considered worthless as soldiers. In all probability their commanders sacrificed them to demonstrate that inadequate officers could also be executed. There is evidence that this was suspected at the time.

The first officer to be executed was Second-Lieutenant Eric Poole of the 11 Battalion West Yorkshire Regiment. He had enlisted in the ranks in 1914 and must have initially impressed, for he was commissioned in 1915. Poole's problems appear to have started during the Battle of the Somme. He was knocked unconscious by a German shell exploding close to him and was evacuated from the trenches suffering from shell-shock. Poole was admitted to a Field Ambulance on 7 July 1916 and from there he was referred to a General Hospital, being admitted on 8 July. At the hospital Captain Clayton of the Medical Corps diagnosed Poole as suffering from shell-shock. He was discharged from here on the 24 July and referred to a convalescent home at Dieppe. At the Dieppe home Poole was examined by Captain Crookshank of the Medical Corps, who noted that Poole's cerebration was slow and that he had a pain in the back. A small myopic astigmatism was also noted. Poole was also seen by a consultant, Sir James Fowler, who found a small irregular cardiac action and certified on 22 August that Poole was still unfit for duty.[92]

Three days later a Medical Board was convened to examine Poole's case and amazingly, considering the consultant's opinion, Lieutenant-Colonel Martin of the

Medical Corps, who presided over the board, recorded that the board found that Poole was fit for duty.[93] Accordingly, Poole was returned to the trenches where, unsurprisingly, he deserted when his unit was ordered to attack the enemy. When he was apprehended the military policeman observed that he was 'confused', and at the trial Captain Armstrong stated that Poole had previously seemed 'rather shaken'.[94] The battalion commander, Lieutenant-Colonel Barker, also gave evidence. His testimony was crushing: 'I knew the accused had been in hospital. I should say he is below the average in intellect. He is rather stupid'.[95] This evidence instantly linked Poole's shell-shock with his low intellect and may have been crucial to the final outcome, the decision to execute him.

Rather unusually, Poole was represented at his trial but unwittingly his 'friend' probably introduced the very evidence that made commutation of his death sentence extremely unlikely. Poole himself told the court:

Since I have had shell shock I, at times, get confused and I have great difficulty in making up my mind. I was in this condition on October 5th [date of his desertion].[96]

Poole went on to claim that he had left his platoon to seek medical help for a 'touch of rheumatism'. Next his representative called Second-Lieutenant Alnwick, who told the court:

when he first came he was rather eccentric. ... I should say he was not fit to have charge of a platoon. He is, in my opinion, more than eccentric. when talking he is apt to wander and not keep to his subject.[97]

Unfortunately this evidence, far from mitigating Poole's case as intended only singled him out as mentally weak and probably made his execution inevitable.

Poole's character assessment then took another, unintentional, turn for the worse when his 'friend' called the battalion's medical officer, Captain Riddell, to give evidence for the defence. Riddell said he had known Poole since May 1916 and continued:

I have always noticed something peculiar in his manner. He is somewhat eccentric and markedly lacking in decision. I think that at times of stress or while under shell fire the accused's mental condition is such that he might very well have great difficulty in coming to any decision and might become so mentally confused that he would not be responsible for his actions.[98]

Then in response to a direct question put to the witness by the court but not recorded Riddell stated: 'The accused is in my opinion more liable to shell-shock than a normal man'.[99] This evidence, designed to help the accused, had the opposite effect. Poole was singled out as different to normal men. The use of the word eccentric to describe Poole was probably a euphemism, perhaps meaning that the defendant was mentally ill. Unfortunately for Poole, to the more senior officers assessing his case it meant unfit.

Poole's representative addressed the court and unwittingly compounded the damage:

I submit that there is something more abnormal in the accused's condition than could be produced by the mere effects of shell-shock. He is more than eccentric and with his poor mental equipment the effect of shell-shock on him is very great. He has been shown by the evidence of the Quartermaster to have been in a very confused state when he came back. I submit that in these circumstances you cannot find that the accused is capable of forming the intention necessary to prove desertion. Mr. Alnwick's evidence clearly shows that before the accused came to France he was what he called 'super eccentric' and I suggest that *this is only a kind word for a severe mental defect.* [my italics][100]

Despite a plea from Poole's brigade commander, Brigadier-General Lambert, to send Poole home, the division, corps and army commanders recommended that the shell-shocked but perhaps abnormal officer be shot. Poole was executed on 10 December 1916.

In many ways Poole was the ideal candidate for a token officer execution. He had suffered previously from shell-shock and was of no further use to the army. Moreover, he was unfit in the eyes of the commanders on account of his mental state. Not only had his personality been denigrated, but he was also said to be prone to the condition of shell-shock. Here was yet another example of a weaker or unfit character being weeded out.

The second officer to be executed was Sub-Lieutenant Edwin Dyett. In fact, his was the first execution of 1917. It is ironic that Dyett had enlisted into the Royal Navy and probably never expected to see trenches, but he was posted to the Royal Naval Division and then sent to the Western Front. His case attracted considerable press attention immediately after his execution and as a result much has been written about this case. Indeed, the central character in the novel *The Secret Battle*, written in 1919 by A. P. Herbert (later an Independent MP for the Universities seat), was probably based on Dyett, the author himself having served in the Royal Naval Division.

Dyett had realised that he was ill-suited to trench warfare and had requested a transfer to sea duties. However, in an attack in November 1916 the division had suffered many casualties and Dyett, who had been held in reserve, was sent forward to join the rest of his battalion. The inevitable happened and in the confusion he was separated from his comrades and made his way to the rear. At his trial a distinguished lawyer represented him, but once again attempts at mitigation only served to worsen the accused's predicament.

Judge Anthony Babington argues that Dyett's defending officer 'seems to have had little skill or experience as a forensic advocate' and only succeeded in eliciting 'replies that must have considerably strengthened the prosecution case.'[101] The defending officer summed up by stating that Dyett was not mentally in control on the day in question and that he was so highly neurotic as to be unfit for service in the field. What was, in actuality, an admission of weak character was recognised by the court, for after sentencing him to death, it recommended mercy partly on the grounds that the prevailing conditions would have seriously affected any young officer 'unless he had a strong character'.[102] But the defence, designed to mitigate Dyett's case and lessen the severity of the final outcome, only highlighted the fact that Dyett was not suited to trench warfare. As the previous cases have shown, nothing was more likely to persuade the top brass to single him out for execution.

A clerk, who witnessed the arrival of the confirmation of the sentence at Brigade Headquarters and processed the relevant papers, noted the general belief that Dyett had been selected for execution as a token officer. Leading Seaman T.

MacMillan, wrote in his diary:

Was he, I wondered, to be the first martyr to the clamour from the ranks for an example to be made of an officer for desertion or cowardice? 'How is it', the men were asking and rightly so, 'that only rankers are being shot for cowardice? How many officers have been guilty of this offence and why have they not been made to answer for it with their lives, as we have to do?' The Higher Command must have heard this grouse grow louder and could not fail to admit the justness of it. If however, they were forced to act, why did they select a mere boy for their first victim?[103]

The answer was that, as in the other cases, Dyett was expendable. He was executed simply because his character was not considered to be strong enough for military service. Why else was his application for a transfer to sea duties, where he could have continued to serve his country, not allowed?

If there was, as MacMillan suggests, a need for the High Command to make an example of one or two officers to show even-handedness, then the selection of two completely shell-shocked victims is surely significant. Far from evoking a sympathetic response, the shell-shock defence had in both cases attracted a condemnation which ultimately proved lethal. Military commanders were not prepared to tolerate soldiers who, in their opinion, did not have the strength of character to withstand trench warfare. Such men were branded 'worthless' without considering whether there were other duties they might be fit to perform. Only five officers received death sentences during the war and the sentence was only confirmed in the cases of the two most junior officers.[104] This in itself suggests that there might have been a class bias operating within the courts martial and the judicial process. That one of those officers executed had risen from the ranks does little to persuade otherwise.

In black and white[1]

Ideas about racial differences and the superiority of one particular race had particular relevance in Britain. At the outbreak of war in 1914 Britain stood at the head of an extensive Empire, the preservation of which had been one of the prime concerns of the eugenists. Racial arguments had been used to explain the supposed superiority of the English over not only the Irish but over other peoples under British rule, particularly in the Indian sub-continent. Indeed, one argument for British rule was the notion that the people of India were unable to govern themselves. It was thought to be the duty of so-called civilised races such as the British export their civilisation to the supposedly more backward races, the notion of the 'White Man's Burden'.

Of necessity the British Army recruited in India and other parts of the Empire, but its attitude towards colonial troops was permeated by racialist as well as imperialist ideas. They were considered inferior, both as soldiers and as people and thought to be incapable of leadership: black soldiers were permitted to become non-commissioned officers but King's commissions were restricted to white British officers only.[2] There was also a great amount of suspicion, particularly in the case of Indians, the reason rooted in the Indian Mutiny of 1857. Since then British units had formed much of the Indian Army to ensure loyalty, but Indian soldiers were segregated from the British. Courts martial records reflect this practice. After the Indian Mutiny many Britons regarded Indians as savages. The bloody massacre of British civilians at Cawnpore was often portrayed as evidence of Indian savagery and perfidy, a further reason why the Indians needed civilising by the supposedly superior Anglo-Saxon race. The ferocity of the response to events at Cawnpore and elsewhere was conveniently overlooked.

Many in Britain wondered if the Indians could be civilised at all. Indians it was felt might revert to barbarity despite the work of missionaries and British administration. In *The Judgement of Dungara* by Rudyard Kipling (1888) a formerly uncivilised tribe is converted by 'a fair white woman' only to regress in an orgy of savagery:

With a bound and a scream there alighted on the rocks above their heads, Nala, once pride of the Mission, a maiden of fourteen summers, good, docile, and virtuous – now naked as the dawn and spitting like a wild-cat.[3]

Even the highly Westernised Wali Dad in Kipling's story *On the City Wall* goes wild during a procession:

His nostrils were distended, his eyes were fixed, and he was smiting himself softly on the breast. The crowd poured by with renewed riot – a gang of Mussulmans hard pressed by some hundred

Hindu fanatics. Wali Dad left my side with an oath, and shouting: 'Ya Hasan! Ya Hussain!' plunged into the thick of the fight, where I lost sight of him.[4]

According to Salman Rushdie, such literature betrayed the attitude that 'Western civilisation has been no more than a veneer; a native remains a native beneath his European jackets and ties. Blood will out'.[5] Notions of Indian degeneracy, believed to be the result of a mixture of blood, were also used to justified British rule.[6] Similarly, Indians were viewed as sexually dubious. Indian males were considered by many to be 'unmanly' and India was portrayed as feminine in the possession of masculine Britain: 'sexual imagery was used to represent not control, but fear of the loss of control'.[7]

In a recent study Kathryn Castle has also shown that in the early years of the twentieth century Indians were portrayed in children's books and periodicals as treacherous savages led by evil usurpers, whilst British figures such as Clive and Warren Hastings were exalted as heroes.[8] So too were Indians who remained loyal to the British. She points out that some authors 'found that the 'steadiness and zeal' of the Sikh could be compared to 'Cromwell's famous Ironsides'.[9] The British ascribed certain traits to various Indian peoples: Sikhs and Jats, for example, were considered 'martial races', in contrast to the Bengalis who were regarded as effeminate.[10]

The Indian Army included both the army raised in India, made up of Indian troops, and the British regiments posted to India. The British proportion was greatly increased after 1857 and a strong military presence retained in India thereafter. The army, whether Indian or British, was always commanded by British officers although some Indians, known as *Wordi* officers, were also commissioned. Certain non-commissioned ranks were also created for Indian troops, such as the *Havildar*, or sergeant. For the purpose of this study references to the Indian Army indicate Indian troops. If reference is made to a British unit serving with the Indian Army, this will be made clear.

India provided about one and a quarter million soldiers for the British Army in the First World War. This is more than any other part of the Empire except Britain itself and represents a higher number than all of the dominions added together.[11] Indeed, more Indians fought in the British Army in the First World War than the aggregate number of Scots, Welsh and Irish. Although the main theatre of war for the Indians was Mesopotamia, where the burden of the action in atrocious conditions fell mainly upon them, many also fought on the Western Front. In fact, after the stalemate of the trenches had set in it was the Indians who made the first breach in the German lines at Neuve Chapelle in northern France during the spring of 1915. Yet the role of the Indians was never truly acknowledged at the time, nor has it been since. A huge and impressive monument to the Indian dead now stands at Neuve. It commemorates thousands of Indians who lost their lives far from home in a war that need not have concerned them.[12] Indeed, the Indians were fighting for a nation that regarded them as uncivilised and inferior, an attitude reflected in the manner in which capital punishment was inflicted on them.

Indians in the army were subject to a particularly harsh code of discipline. This was another consequence of the Indian Mutiny, memories of which persisted in early twentieth century military minds. The worst incident of the mutiny was probably at Cawnpore, where the British garrison surrendered in return for safe passage and the safety of the civilian occupants of the town. After the garrison surrendered its weapons the Indian rebels massacred civilians as well as troops. Retribution was swift and the atrocities committed by the British relief force matched, if not surpassed, those of the Indians. Exaggerated stories of Indian atrocities left the British with an 'obsessive fear of savage Indian men raping helpless English women'.[13] The events of this mutiny and the manner in which it was remembered by the British explain why another Indian mutiny, this time in Singapore in 1915, resulted in the largest mass execution of the war.

No register has survived of the courts martial of Indian soldiers. The India Office holds no such records. If a record was kept at all then it must have been separate to those of the British Army, including British units serving in the Indian Army. This segregation of records typified the British approach. The only surviving references to Indian executions are those in personal and battalion diaries. These tend only to refer to executions and contain few details of death sentences not carried out. It is therefore impossible to analyse the relationship between death sentences and executions of Indians.

Field-Marshal Haig visited the headquarters of the Indian Corps on 29 November 1914 and found it to be in a state of despondency. He was shocked to find British and native clerks working in the same rooms, and furthermore:

There was one particularly large room in which there were three large and long tables arranged for a meal. I was told that three officers' messes (including the Corps Commanders) were accommodated in this room, and that all cooked in the same kitchen. I came away feeling that things were not altogether in an efficient state in the Indian Corps...[14]

What probably shocked Haig so much was that the segregation of British and Indians, believed to be necessary to the maintenance of discipline, had lapsed in the cramped conditions.

Segregation of Indians and British usually continued even after death. Burials of Indian soldiers killed in action were normally confined to a corner of any given cemetery. Often Indians were buried in separate cemeteries. Burial arrangements are typified by one particular cemetery near Péronne in the Somme Department of France. Although theoretically one cemetery, known as La Chapelette British and Indian Cemetery, it is in actuality divided in two with the majority of the Indians buried in a separate area to the British. Those Indians who were Christian are buried in another part of the British zone of the cemetery.

Thus, one cannot know accurately how many Indian troops were sentenced to death or executed. This has led to a slightly confused picture of some events where no official record exists. It is not helpful to speculate, but the overall impression is that the Indians were treated particularly badly by the courts martial and it appears likely, from the surviving fragments of evidence, that most death sentences were carried out.

The largest traceable execution of Indians followed the mutiny in Singapore in 1915. The mutineers ran through the streets of Singapore killing any European on sight: in all, thirty-nine people were killed. The cause of the mutiny remains obscure. The British report blamed poor leadership and nationalist propagandists aided by German intriguers, but there is also evidence that the Muslim troops were uneasy about fighting against 'the head of their religion, i.e. the Sultan at Stamboul.'[15] According to Martin Gilbert thirty-seven mutineers were executed in Singapore by firing squad and a further eighteen militants were hanged in India.[16] Other evidence suggests that the actual number could be higher. A. H. Dickinson, an officer cadet of the Straits Settlement Police, recorded in his diary that 212 mutineers were found guilty, one other was acquitted. Of these, forty-seven were executed, according to his diary.[17] Gilbert incorrectly states that the mutineers were Sikhs, when in fact they were Muslim and a detachment from 36 Sikh Regiment helped to suppress the mutiny.[18]

Other executions of Indian troops can be traced in diaries held at the Imperial War Museum. Lieutenant Gell was a Regimental Signal Officer with 69 Punjabi Regiment in Aden who records in his diary the following events:

Monday 28th December 1914. 4 Pathans deserted from 27th Punjabis 1 day before yesterday + were caught by cavalry yesterday going in enemy's direction. Some have gone from 128th Pioneers at Ismaila too. Someone is getting at them + telling them they have taken a circle round from India + that their homes are really quite near here. Hope these fellows are shot as an example.'
'Saturday 2nd January 1915. Three of the four deserters of 27th were shot on Thursday morning + one was commuted to penal servitude for life. They took it perfectly calmly I believe.[19]

This shows how much more harshly the Indians were treated than British soldiers were. Three out of four were executed, far higher than the normal eleven per cent average of executions carried out on troops recorded in the registers. Additionally, the one soldier who had his death sentence commuted was sentenced to penal servitude for life. The normal sentence upon commutation of the death penalty at this stage of the war was five years penal servitude or two years hard labour. Occasionally, a British soldier received ten years penal servitude. Penal servitude for life was not imposed on British soldiers until much later in the war when commuted sentences generally appeared to get harsher, and even then it was still rare.

Another Indian execution, this time on the Western Front, was recorded in the diary of Captain T. H. Westmacott, the Assistant Provost Marshall of 1 Indian Cavalry Division.

On 26 June, 1916, a *Sowar* in the 29 Lancers shot the *Wordi Major* of the regiment dead. He then threw away his rifle, tore off most of his clothes, and rushed off to the HQ of the Lucknow Brigade, where he happened to catch General Morton Gage, the Brigadier, in the street. He told the General a long story, but the General could not understand a word. The man, wrote Westmacott, was a Delhi policeman, and a jat, who had enlisted for the period of the war. He was a sulky kind of fellow, but there was no doubt in Westmacott's mind that the *wordi major*, who was in his opinion an absolute rotter, had goaded the fellow to desperation.[20]

The man was shot by a firing squad on 21 July at Doullons and, as he faced the firing squad he shouted in Hindustani to his (Indian) executioners, Hindus and Muslims alike, that there was no justice in the British *Sirkar*. He had done as he had done because he had been abused, and he called upon all those who had been similarly abused to do the same, only they should kill themselves rather than be shot.[21]

Apparently, he was not killed outright by the firing squad and so Westmacott had the gruesome task of administering a *coup de grace* with his revolver.

There is in fact one recorded sentence against an Indian soldier in the official records. Whether this was inadvertently written into a British register or whether the individual was serving with a British unit at the time is not clear. Private Din Iman was serving with the Mule Company (and therefore could conceivably be attached to a British regiment) when he deserted. On 4 April 1916 he was sentenced to thirty lashes.[22] There is no other record of an Indian court martial for capital offences or otherwise. What is especially interesting about this one case is that the sentence of 30 lashes is one that could not legally have been inflicted on a British soldier. That particular punishment had been abolished in the British Army in 1881 because of its inhumane nature. Of course, what was deemed inhumane for a British soldier did not necessarily count, in British military circles, as inhumane for an Indian soldier. This is a clear and unambiguous example of how double standards were applied.

In the absence of official records there is absolutely no way of knowing exactly how many Indians were executed or even sentenced to death but reprieved. What evidence we have tends to suggest that death sentences on Indians were rarely commuted and that when they were the resulting sentence was harsh.

Unlike the Indians, details of Afro-Caribbean soldiers in the British Army were recorded in the registers of courts martial, which makes a reasonable analysis of their experience with British military justice possible. The most striking feature about death sentences passed on men serving in African and West Indian regiments is that though there was a relatively low number of condemnations, the proportion of executions of these black soldiers was high.

In the British West Indies Regiment, for example, there were eight death sentences, four of which were carried out. Two of the executions were for murder. The first involved eighteen year-old Private James Mitchell who was condemned to death for the attempted rape of a woman in Palestine and the murder of her husband. He was executed on 22 December 1917.[23] The second, Private Albert Denny, was convicted by General Court Martial in Taranto, Italy of the murder of a comrade whilst drunk. He was executed on 20 January 1920.[24] The two other executions of West Indian soldiers were Private Hubert Clarke, shot for striking a senior officer and using violence towards a military policemen whom he attacked with a razor, in Egypt in 1917,[25] and seventeen year-old Private Herbert Morris from St. Catherine, Jamaica. Morris was executed for desertion on the Western Front in September 1917.[26] Of the remaining death sentences, which were commuted to various terms of penal servitude, two were for striking senior officers, one for mutiny and another for sleeping on post. This is most revealing because half of the condemnations on West Indian soldiers involved some form of dissent or resistance to authority. Unfortunately the circumstances of each offence will remain unknown, but it is clear that British courts martial dealt severely with any resistance to British authority in colonial units.

There were two death sentences passed on men serving with the Nigerian Regiment, both in East Africa. The first, Private Samuel Sabongidda, convicted of using violence towards a senior officer, was executed on 27 July 1917.[27] The second, Private Ibadan, had his death sentence for cowardice commuted to fourteen years penal servitude; a harsh sentence by comparison with white British units.[28] Three out of the nine death sentences on soldiers in the Gold Coast Regiment were

Men of the British West Indies Regiment on the Western Front

carried out. Private Aziberi Frafra was executed in East Africa during 1916 for casting away his arms.[29] The following year Private Mamprusi was shot for desertion, also in East Africa.[30] Private Dezari Barrana (also spelt as Bossana or Barama) was convicted of murder in 1918, but his sentence was not confirmed. Unfortunately for him he was convicted again in a retrial and executed.[31] The other condemnations against men in the Gold Coast Regiment involved offences of sleeping on post and cowardice; all were commuted to terms of penal servitude ranging from five to fourteen years.[32] Once again these are harsher sentences than those usually confirmed for white soldiers.

There were three death sentences passed on men in the West African Regiment. One of these was carried out. Private Fatoma was executed on 19 July 1915 in Cameroon for the offence of cowardice and quitting his post. In his defence he claimed that in the darkness he had been lost by his patrol and not vice versa. There was no evidence to contradict this version of events but, despite the possibility of doubt, the sentence was confirmed.[33] The case was not reviewed by any senior officers and the file went straight from the court martial to the Commander-in-Chief. It appears that the confirmation was never in question. The only other example of a sentence being confirmed without any intermediate recommendations was the case of Private Davis who was executed on 2 July 1915 at Gallipoli. Davis, it may be recalled, was an Irishman serving with the Royal Munster Fusiliers.

The involvement of men from the colonies was not restricted to soldiers. Indeed, an often overlooked contribution to the war effort was that of the labour companies

107

whose role, on the face of it at least, appears to be less prominent than that of the fighting soldiers. This, however, does not do justice to the labourers who performed a vital task in conditions every bit as exacting as that of the soldiers: many carried out their duties under enemy fire and many became casualties (over 50,000 labourers were killed on the Western Front alone). The expansion of the British Army from a six division expeditionary force to a mass army of a modern type brought with it an increasing supply problem. The acquisition of more and larger artillery added to the burden. The expansion of the army was therefore matched by an expansion of the Labour Corps. Insufficient manpower was available in Britain, but the Empire provided an obvious pool of recruits who could be trained to perform what were initially considered to be the more menial tasks involved with transportation of supplies. The value of skilled labourers to perform tasks such as railway building soon became apparent, even if the army was not particularly successful in its attempts to muster specialist workers. The largest contribution to the Labour Corps came from Egypt, where more than a quarter of a million men were recruited. A further 477,000 labourers were enlisted from other parts of Africa. Most served with the army in Africa, but some were transported to the Western Front. However, the Western Front was primarily the domain of the Chinese and Indian Labour Corps, who provided 175,000 and 58,000 men respectively. Native or black labour was granted a lowly status by the British who regarded these workers as camp followers. They were employed on fixed contracts rather than being enlisted in a military sense. As such they were subject to military discipline but not to summary punishments. In theory at least they could only be punished if found guilty by a court martial. Native labourers were segregated from their white counterparts. They were placed under the supervision of European officers and NCOs and subject to other restrictions. Most significant was the ban on alcohol and the prohibition of contact with white women. Clearly, black labourers (a term that included Chinese) were not trusted by their British masters. Not surprisingly serious disturbances broke out and many labourers were repatriated in early 1918.

Fourteen Chinese labourers were sentenced to death by courts martial on the Western Front. Eleven sentences were confirmed, all for murder, although only ten executions were actually carried out, because one coolie committed suicide to avoid the firing squad. The three Chinese whose sentences were commuted included two who had been convicted of striking senior officers and one further murderer whose sentence was commuted to penal servitude for life. Another example which shows that the Chinese were subject to a harsher version of British military justice can be found in an order issued in May 1919 stating that the Suspension of Sentences Act, which allowed commanders to keep the convicted person 'in the field' so to speak, did not apply to the Chinese.[34] Any convicted Chinese had to serve out his sentence.

Unsurprisingly, given the nature of the restrictions placed on them, the Chinese labourers appear to have fared particularly badly when their crimes involved white prostitutes or alcohol. Neither circumstance was likely to elicit a favourable hearing from a British court martial. Three Chinese labourers were sentenced to death for the murder of a prostitute and her three children. Two were executed on 15 January 1919 and the third committed suicide.[35] A further two were executed for the mur-

Chinese labourers on the Western Front under the watchful eye of a British NCO

der of another prostitute in Belgium. Coolies K'ung Ch'ing Hsing and Hei Chi Ming were executed in early 1920 for the wounding of two French prostitutes and the murder of a British Army sergeant at a brothel near Le Havre.[36] Significantly, the British Army records only list the men's identities as Coolies nos. 44340 and 97171; the names have been obtained from other sources. Other Chinese labourers who were executed appear to have murdered fellow labourers following squabbles over debts or alleged extortion. These were probably the result of another vice often ascribed to the Chinese, gambling.

In addition to 1,400,000 soldiers, India also supplied 55,000 labourers, 12,000 porters and 1,200 grooms for the British war effort. Again there is no surviving record of courts martial involving these men. It can only be assumed that, as with the Indian Army, a separate register was maintained which has not survived. There are no diary records of executions of Indian labourers as we have for Indian soldiers, yet it remains unlikely that there were no courts martial at all. How many of these courts martial resulted in a death sentence or an actual execution cannot be ascertained from existing sources.

However, records do exist of the courts martial of other labourers, including death sentences passed on five Egyptian labourers (three were after 1920), one of which resulted in execution. The death sentences were mainly for murder. The execution arose out of a mutiny by some five hundred Egyptian labourers at the port of Marseilles on 16 September 1917. The disorder was suppressed with the aid of

Indian troops but not before one labourer, Mohammed Ahmed, had assaulted a British officer and seized his rifle.[37] Other Egyptians overpowered the mutineer but the British court, sitting on 28 September, still took a dim view of the incident. Mohamed Ahmed was sentenced to death for using violence towards the officer and was shot twelve days later.[38] There is one other recorded death sentence on a labourer, this time in the Black Sea Labour Company. This was also for murder and resulted in execution.[39]

Three men serving with the Cape Coloured Labour Company, all from Cape Town in South Africa, were sentenced to death on the Western Front in 1919. All had their sentences carried out. Privates Abraham Davids and Peter Harris were convicted of the murder of a Belgian prostitute.[40] Nineteen year-old Private Alberts was executed for desertion.[41] Clearly there was little tolerance of crime committed by black labourers and soldiers alike. Many of the cases involved murder, but it is interesting to note that hardly any of these death sentences passed for murder were commuted.

Attitudes towards the native labourers were often influenced by presupposed racial characteristics. For instance, the British Army was fearful of the reaction of black men to white women. This applied particularly to contact with prostitutes and less leniency was shown to labourers, or soldiers, from the colonies who were indicted for murder than was generally allowed for their white comrades. Equally, black soldiers and labourers alike were not thought to be capable of leadership and had white officers imposed upon them. This was consistent with the pervasive view that such races were incapable of self-government often cited as justification for the Empire itself. To what extent the prohibition of contact with white women had contributed to the problem can only be supposed. The issue of control and authority, seemingly so important to the army, took on its most brutal form in relation to the native labour corps leading one historian to remark, 'the traits ascribed to Oriental labour form an uncanny mirror image of the perceived social character of the working class [in Edwardian Britain] sharpened by a rampant racism'.[42]

Military law was not restricted to the army and labourers. As well as civilians who came under military law in occupied areas, prisoners of war could also be tried by courts martial. Six Turkish prisoners of war were sentenced to death for murder and four of them executed. The identity of the victims remains unclear; it is possible that they were British soldiers. The method of execution was not the military style firing squad but hanging. This may suggest a lower status granted to Turkish prisoners: the firing squad was the accepted form of execution for soldiers. This is even more disturbing when contrasted with the treatment of German prisoners of war convicted of similar offences.

British courts martial sentenced three German prisoners to death, but none was executed. On 5 July 1916, a German prisoner, named as Hauptmann, was convicted of killing British soldiers by exploding a bomb after surrendering.[43] Earlier in the war, on 17 March 1915, Gefreiter [Lance-Corporal] Manneinfeld was convicted of a similar act, firing at British soldiers after surrendering.[44] Neither death sentence was confirmed by the Commander-in-Chief, in the former case Douglas Haig and in the latter, John French. A third German soldier, sentenced to death for striking a British officer, had his sentence commuted to one year's hard labour. There was clearly reluctance on the part of two separate British Field-Marshals to have a

German prisoner executed, a reluctance not extended to Turks.

In Britain Turks were not considered to be of high racial status. There were a number of features which might have been held against them. Firstly, Turks were identified as Muslims rather than Christians. They were on the fringe of Europe and their political and military power was thought to be diminishing. Turks were considered less civilised and the treatment of the prisoners taken at Kut-al-Amara could have done nothing to contradict this view. In John Buchan's highly popular novel *Greenmantle* (1916) the Turkish government is portrayed as backward and corrupt, in other words incapable of self-rule. The country is portrayed as uncivilised and in a state of decline with a population that 'didn't look as if they understand any *civilised* tongue' [my italics].[45] Moreover, the degeneration of the Turks is portrayed as being the consequence of a mixture of races:

But it was the rabble that caught the eye – very wild pinched, miserable rabble. I never in my life saw such swarms of beggars, and you walked down that street to the accompaniment of entreaties for alms in all the tongues of the Tower of Babel.[46]

Germans on the other hand, as well as being generally lighter in skin tone, were Christian. Moreover, many were protestant. Anglo-Saxonism could easily be extended to include Germans: the 'fair white woman' of Kipling's *The Judgement of Dungara*, was a German. There also appears to have been a genuine respect between German and British soldiers. Siegfried Sassoon looked on some dead Germans he encountered in a trench during the Battle of the Somme with sympathy, adding:

In the blear beginning of daylight they seemed as much the victims of a catastrophe as the men who had attacked them. As I stepped over one of the Germans an impulse made me lift him up from the miserable ditch. Propped against the bank, his blond face was undisfigured, except by the mud which I wiped from his eyes and mouth with my coat sleeve. He'd evidently been killed while digging, for his tunic was knotted loosely about his shoulders. He didn't look to be more than eighteen.[47]

This respect was reciprocated. Throughout his book *The Storm of Steel* the German writer Ernst Jünger tells of his admiration for the British (by which he includes Dominion troops), saying of a British officer who commanded an Indian unit:

If these lines are read by any one belonging to the 1st Hariana Lancers I wish to express to him in this place my respect for a body of men who could claim as their commander such a one as he whom I had the honour to fight.[48]

Whilst this might be suggestive of a romantic view of war it should be noted that both writers relate stories of brutality between British and German troops, especially in the heat of battle. Jünger quite coldly justifies the shooting of surrendering British soldiers in 1918 as 'a baseness'.[49]

The final outcome of cases involving prisoners of war, just like those of labourers, often depended on British preconceptions about race, its ascribed traits and, more importantly, the status of the race in question. North European or white soldiers, labourers and prisoners of war clearly fared better at courts martial and with the Commander-in-Chief than did those from supposedly black races. Certain misdemeanours seem to stand out amongst the charges brought against black soldiers and labourers, namely offences against women and against authority. Was this a true reflection of the nature of the crimes committed by men from these colonial units? In all likelihood it is more a reflection of ascribed racial traits and other concerns of the British Army. Regulations had been designed to prevent these very crimes. It is surely more likely that the executions for these types of crime were simply a continuation of measures put in place to deal with the pre-existing assumptions about black soldiers and labourers. When comparisons are made between white soldiers charged with similar offences a more lenient approach can be detected, with fewer executions carried out: ten men were executed for the murder of civilians (all women) but only one of these men was white.[50] Unfortunately, records of victims where the death penalty was not carried out have not survived and it is impossible to tell whether the victims were civilians or other soldiers. Therefore, no comparison of reprieves is possible, but it appears that the ratio of nine black to one white murder cannot be realistic. The harsh authoritarian approach adopted in dealing with men from the colonies actually helped to shape their response, which was characterised by occasional violent reaction to British authority. Similarly, British fears about how colonial troops and labourers would react to white women ensured that any response by the British authorities was harsh.

The final judgement

The role of the Commander-in-Chief

How important was the role of the Commander-in-Chief? Individuals such as Haig have often associated with the disasters of the war and this applies as much to executions as to the conduct of the war itself. Field-Marshal Haig's confirmation of over 250 death sentences is often seen a consistent with his popular reputation as 'the butcher of the Somme'. The implication here is that Haig cared little about the men in his charge, that his command was characterised by high casualties and many executions. The evidence suggests, however, that at least in terms of the death penalty this reputation applies to Haig no more so than it does to the other Commanders-in-Chief. What exactly then was the contribution of Sir Douglas Haig, and for that matter Sir John French and the other Commanders-in-Chief?

Both John French and Douglas Haig held traditional military beliefs, insisting for instance that strict maintenance of discipline would give their army moral superiority over the enemy.[1] This attitude was far from unique: it was reputed that General Allenby once berated a soldier for being improperly dressed, only to discover the man to be dead.[2] As we have already seen, both French and Haig showed a ready willingness to apply the death penalty when they held the post of Commander-in-Chief. Haig openly stated his faith in the deterrent value of capital punishment.[3]

The Commander-in-Chief confirmed approximately eleven per cent of all death sentences; the remainder were either commuted or not confirmed. Some were quashed, presumably because there was doubt as to their legality. When civilian death sentences are added, the percentage of executions rises to approximately thirteen per cent, indicating that civilians under military rule were treated far more harshly than soldiers. The role of the Commander-in-Chief is therefore, not only crucial, but also extremely revealing of attitudes in the British Army.

The British Army had separate Commanders-in-Chief for each theatre of the war. At Gallipoli the Commander-in-Chief was General Sir Ian Hamilton. On the Western Front, where approximately ninety-per cent of the death sentences were passed, the Commander-in-Chief from August 1914 until the end of 1915 was John French; thereafter it was Douglas Haig, who confirmed a total of 253 death sentences. As GOC 1 Army during French's period of overall command, Haig had recommended many more death sentences. Quite naturally any examination of the Commander-in-Chief's role will focus upon Haig, though detailed comparison of the two commanders reveals little difference in the degree of severity they showed. A total of 684 death sentences were referred to French when Commander-in-Chief, seventy-five (roughly eleven-per cent) were confirmed. After Haig had replaced French as Commander-in-Chief, a colossal 2,580 death sentences were passed with 359 (just under fourteen per cent) confirmed. Some of these were post-war cases, mainly in Egypt. Initially, this may suggest that Haig was more likely to confirm death sentences than French, however, a close examination of the circumstances makes such a view untenable.

Available figures do not give a fair and balanced picture for three reasons. Firstly, the number of civilians coming before military courts rose dramatically in the later stages of the war and, as they were more likely to be executed than soldiers, this has affected the statistics, especially those relating to Haig's command. Some of these figures relate to the post-war period when martial law was enforced in Egypt and Turkey with a large degree of severity. Indeed, if the civilians are removed from the analysis, then the percentage of confirmations of soldiers only, drops significantly for both commanders: French's to just over nine per cent and Haig's to twelve and three-quarters. Secondly, the army Haig commanded was many times the size of that for which French had responsibility. With a larger army came many more problems of logistics, and with granting leave, all likely to upset morale if things went wrong, as indeed they occasionally did. Finally, the war fought during the Haig period was a rather different one than under French. A feature of the latter half of the war was the large-scale set piece battles of the Somme and Ypres. Poison gas was also used with more regularity. All of this made the Western Front a rather different and less attractive place, where desertion was more likely.

Direct comparison between the two commanders is impossible. Therefore, it is far more satisfactory to examine the office of Commander-in-Chief and not concentrate on any individual. It is also preferable to concentrate on the executions within the army and leave the civilians, who often fell under the jurisdiction of other Commanders-in-Chief, to one side. The civilians[4] were also from disparate parts of the war zones and circumstances were often very different making any attempt at analysis an extremely complicated affair.

In earlier chapters comparisons were made between soldiers of the various countries where the British Army was recruited. A similar approach here shows that the Commander-in-Chief was remarkably consistent in confirming death sentences. In the cases of the English, Scottish, Welsh, Irish, Canadian and South African troops approximately ninety per cent of death sentences were commuted, the remaining ten per cent were executed. Significantly, the Commander-in-Chief treated the Irish in much the same way as the English, Scots and slightly better than the Welsh. (Interestingly, the execution of one soldier in every ten condemnations was a long established military tradition with its origins in the Roman army, but there is no evidence that the Commander-in-Chief deliberately followed such a policy of decimation and there was certainly nothing in British military law to legitimise it if he had.) Nonetheless, there were two exceptions to the general pattern: the Australians, whose regulations forbade any executions, and the New Zealanders for whom the proportion of executions was approximately twenty-two per cent (for ease of reference all this statistical information has been reproduced in tabular form in the appendix).

The Australian sample is easily explained: no executions of Australian troops were permitted and all Australian death sentences were commuted or quashed. This was not true of the New Zealand soldiers though. It appears that a New Zealand soldier was twice as likely to have his death sentence confirmed than a British, Canadian or South African. Australian immunity from execution has much to do with this. Australians and New Zealanders fought in the same corps and were to all intents and purposes, treated as one unit. In fact, two of the five New Zealanders executed were Australians who had enlisted in the New Zealand Army. It could be argued, therefore, that New Zealand troops paid the price for Australian immunity. Paradoxically, therefore, the two exceptions to the trend of one confirmation in every ten death sentences do little to undermine it.

Haig persistently tried to gain authority to execute Australians because he believed discipline to be particularly bad in the Australian units. In a letter to his wife, dated 28 February 1918, he wrote:

I spent some time today with the Canadians. They are really fine disciplined soldiers now and so smart and clean. I am sorry to say that the Australians are not nearly so efficient. I put this down to Birdwood [the commander of the Australian Imperial Force], who, instead of facing the problem, has gone in for the easier way of saying everything is perfect and making himself as popular as possible. We have to separate the Australians into Convalescent Camps of their own, because they were giving so much trouble when along with our men and put such revolutionary ideas into their heads.[5]

Field-Marshal Haig also came to the defence of the New Zealand commander, General Godley, who was being compared unfavourably to General Birdwood, commander of the Australian troops. Haig recorded in his diary for 3 March 1918 that he had been sent a graph showing there to be a greater proportion of Australians held in prisons than any other troops. He commented:

That is to say, nearly one Australian in every hundred men is in prison. This is greatly due to the fact that the Australian refuses to allow capital punishment to be awarded to any Australian. Before we introduced the 'suspended sentence' in February, 1915, the British had 5.1 men per thousand in prison. By June that year the numbers fell to 1.2 and in August to .7 per thousand. Really the absence of crime in this Army is quite wonderful.[6]

This reveals Haig's faith in the deterrent value of the death penalty. It also shows that he was aware that statistics could be used to draw comparisons between the different armies under his command. In this context, the Commander-in-Chief's consistency is not so surprising: Haig was profoundly aware of the importance of these statistics for his post-war reputation. The consistency was no coincidence.

It is difficult to draw firm conclusions about Haig's treatment of the French-speaking Canadians. After the mutinies of 1917, Haig held a low opinion of the fighting abilities of the French soldiers – he was reluctant for the Americans to be attached to the French Army as he believed this was a 'waste of valuable troops'[7] – but his feelings about French-Canadians are unknown. Thirty-five out of the 218 Canadians sentenced to death (mostly in the Haig era) can be identified as belonging to French-speaking units. Of these, six were executed (seventeen per cent). However, five of these men were from the same unit: they were executed at the insistence of their own battalion commander.[8]

The most important feature of the role of the Commander-in-Chief in relation to death sentences was as final arbiter. As such, there was little difference between any of the Commanders-in-Chief. Examining the role of the generals does not add anything to the ongoing criticism of Haig. On the contrary, in the context of executions, Haig's command is synonymous with consistency and, above all, even-handedness. His record is comparable to that of his predecessor and it seems likely that he acted no differently than any other senior British officer would have.

The disproportionate number of Irish soldiers executed (commensurate with their actual numbers) owes nothing to Haig, or to French. The Commander-in-Chief appears to have displayed a remarkable consistency in confirmations and this was extended to the Irish. The disproportionate number of Irish soldiers condemned to death was a feature of sentencing at courts martial level. This was carried over into the number of executions, but not caused by any action taken by the Commander-in-Chief. Haig and French both showed consistency in their actions and have almost identical records in relation to Irish executions.

However, the notion that an individual such as Haig or French was singularly responsible for deciding who was executed, when, and where, is nonsense. It is highly unlikely that the Commander-in-Chief actually read the courts martial papers of each and every case that he confirmed, let alone all those he was required to consider: he had a war to run after all. In the vast majority of cases the role of the Commander-in-Chief must, of necessity, have been to authorize a decision already made elsewhere. That decision, probably made in the Personal Services Branch, was an outcome formed by a number of concerns, ideas and beliefs. Recommendations made by senior officers no doubt carried much weight; so too did disciplinary concerns. These considerations often outweighed the merits of individual cases. The evidence also suggests that attitudes, ascribed traits and prejudice – mostly formed before 1914 – played an important part in the whole process by which individuals were picked out from the large number of death sentences passed.

Coupled with this was the wider power to order executions enjoyed by the British Commanders-in-Chief compared to other armies and a greater acceptance of the death penalty as a deterrent in Britain. Most British commanders believed in the efficacy of the death penalty. Junior officers, sitting on courts martial also believed in it and sentenced over 3,000 British soldiers to death. The evidence supports the view that capital punishment was considered a vital weapon in the maintenance of discipline, accounting for the increase in death sentences as the army prepared for an offensive. The death sentence was employed not as a reactive measure to what happened on the battlefield but as part of a coherent and carefully considered disciplinary code underpinning the authority of the High Command.

By 1918, however, something had changed. The death sentence, although not abandoned, is certainly less evident. It was no longer used as a means of enforcing discipline before an offensive, and it appears that one significant reason for this was the altered state of the army. Like the French and German armies, the British Army had become a conscripted one. As such, its leaders had to accept the responsibility for placing conscripts in the firing line, men who had not chosen to accept King's Regulations. Recourse to the death sentence became less frequent.

The army was continually evolving. It had become unrecognisable militarily by 1918, but many pre-war social concerns and fears persisted. They had an important influence on the army and helped to shape the manner by which the courts martial selected men for the ultimate penalty. Fears of racial degeneration, an important belief amongst the pre-war British professional classes, spanned the political spectrum. Popular writers with political views as diverse as Arthur Conan-Doyle and H. G. Wells wrote about degeneration in some form or another. Eugenists believed in the necessity of intervention to stop racial degeneration. Intervention usually came in the form of segregation of degenerates from the rest of society, to prevent their procreation.

Closely related to these beliefs were concerns about immigration, in particular Jewish and Irish immigration, which were believed to be degrading the English stock as well as importing such alien problems as violence and idleness. In Britain, it was the Irish who aroused the greatest fear, not only because of a belief in their perfidious nature, exacerbated by the violence of Fenianism, but also because of the large numbers of poor Irish who settled the large industrial cities where degeneration was believed to be most acute. Fears of the Irish hastening social decline within England therefore fused with concerns about Irish loyalty to create a volatile cocktail of anti-Irish feeling.

The Boer War and the ensuing recruitment crisis, not only provided a new and urgent platform for the eugenists, but it also brought the issue firmly to the attention of the army. If the army had remained aloof from the fears of degeneration before the Boer War it could not hope to afterwards. The British Army was placed firmly in the public spotlight and recruitment needs during the First World War did nothing to ease the concerns. Indeed, if anything, fears were enhanced. Senior commanders felt fear for their own reputations. Their sense of vulnerability focused their concerns onto the quality of the men under their command. It is in this context that we must now see the executions during the First World War.

Before the Boer War the army had been regarded as the protector of the British Empire. To many, the future of the Empire had depended on the superiority of the English race and the efficiency of the military. Both concepts had been severely mauled: the quality of the race was openly questioned and the army had struggled to defeat an ill-equipped force of farmers. The Boer War had shaken the British people's confidence in its security. Historically, Britain had relied on naval dominance for defence but, by 1914, with the growth of the German navy, confidence that the Empire could be preserved through British sea power alone was crumbling. Concerns grew that the Royal Navy might not even be able to defend the motherland, fuelling stories of German invasions. In this atmosphere of fear, British generals felt they had every reason to doubt the quality of their working-class troops.

Events of the First World War did nothing to allay those fears. The inability of the British Army to stem the German advance and then to push the German Army back became increasingly worrying for commanders and politicians alike. The quality of the British soldier became a growing cause for concern, so too did the problem of desertion in the face of the enemy. The army's ignorance of psychosomatic medicine also created problems in dealing with the large and unprecedented numbers of shell-shock cases. The sufferers were too readily castigated as malingerers or as worthless men. Without doubt, many of the soldiers executed were victims of this misunderstood mental condition.

Another concern for the commanders, although hardly exclusive to them, was the feeling that the best and bravest men were being killed by the thousand whilst the degenerates survived. In this context, it is not surprising that some commanders attempted to purge the ranks of the unfit. Closely related to this was the fear that supposedly weaker soldiers would infect the rest of the army. Therefore, some commanders recommended clearing out those identified as weak before they could have any damaging effect on the others and there are ample examples of commanders recommending an execution on these very grounds. This amounted to a sort of front-line eugenics whereby senior officers sought to prevent the unfit from infecting the rest of the army, or the healthy body. In a country with a strong tradition of capital punishment, it is not surprising that part of the intervention sought by the army commanders should be the frequent use of the firing squad. Far from being a phenomenon of the military or an anachronistic army practice, the use of the death penalty was very much a part of British culture at that time.

Notions of British, or more accurately English, superiority meant that soldiers, and ultimately civilians, were treated according to their racial ranking. The first to suffer on this account were clearly the Irish who, despite their loyalty to the British Army, were sentenced to death and ultimately executed at a far higher rate than would be expected in relation to their actual numbers. This was caused, not by any overtly anti-Irish policy pursued by the Commander-in-Chief, but by the prevailing belief that the Irish were inferior and untrustworthy. This was not solely an anti-Catholic prejudice, although this is undeniably an important element. It was applied more generally to the Irish as a people, whatever their religion. For this reason, the mainly Protestant soldiers of the Ulster units fared no better than Irish Catholics from the south. There was a general view that all the Irish were inferior and indisciplined.

Soldiers from the colonies were also treated according to British ideas about their racial status and ascribed characteristics. Indian soldiers were segregated from British soldiers, even to the point where courts martial records were kept separately, if at all. That records of British courts martial have survived whilst the Indian ones have not is no surprise in the context of the small regard afforded to the Indian troops by their British commanders. Even the military achievements of the Indians, fighting in a war that need not have concerned them and in conditions that were entirely alien to them, have never been truly acknowledged. The word Indian was synonymous with mutinous and savage. Consequently, Indian soldiers were regarded during the First World War as inferior.

There is no way of even estimating with any expectation of accuracy exactly how many Indians were executed. However, there is enough evidence to suggest that a significant number were executed, and not solely as a result of the Singapore mutiny. There is no need for unhelpful speculation. The lack of any record of Indian courts martial is eloquent testimony to the British Command's lack of respect for the Indian soldier, which was reflected in the literature of Kipling and in adventure periodicals. There is even evidence of the administering of lashes to at least one Indian soldier, a practice considered too barbaric as a punishment for British soldiers.

Other colonial troops also appear to have come off rather badly from their brush with British military justice, although there are insufficient numbers to make any analysis of individual countries wholly satisfactory. When viewed as a whole, however, it is clear that black soldiers and Chinese labourers were subject to different, and harsher, treatment than British troops. The harsher treatment of those believed to be racially inferior was even extended to Turkish prisoners of war, but never to German prisoners.

The executions themselves, and the process of selection, were reflections of pre-war British attitudes. They do not represent the will of any one individual such as Haig, but were products of a far more general belief about race and heredity and class. This attitude remained a pervasive one long after the war ended and certainly influenced the findings of the Southborough Committee of Enquiry into Shell-Shock. The committee found that Jews, the Irish and city-dwellers were all more likely to break down when under fire than others. What this really represented was a confirmation that these groups had been singled out as poor soldiers. Not surprisingly, it was these same groups of people who were considered degenerate before the war. The Southborough Committee's report can therefore be regarded as representing continuity of belief spanning the pre-war period and persisting throughout the war and beyond.

In this context, it is surprising that the number of executions was not far greater. It may be the case that ninety-per cent of the death sentences were commuted largely because the Commander-in-Chief was benign, but this seems unlikely. Haig, the final arbiter in the majority of the cases, was a firm believer in the deterrent value of the death penalty and was not afraid to say so in his diary. He may have been concerned about the questions being asked by the Labour MP, Philip Snowden, and this might have suppressed the use of the firing squad, but this is impossible to measure. It is more likely that the need to keep as many men as possible in the field of battle was the most influential factor, which also explains the introduction of the Suspension of Sentences Act in 1915.

However, there remained some soldiers who simply were of no use to the army. These included shell-shocked individuals such as the two officers, Dyett and Poole and the worthless and weaker soldiers, the degenerate and the unmanly. All were singled out and shot. Like the Irish, they too were the targets of the pre-war concern with degeneracy, itself a result of industrial and imperial anxieties in a post-Darwinian age. These concerns continued into the war and remained firmly in place when the war ended.

Appendix

Comparative tables

Figure 4: Traceable Death Sentences
Numbers of condemnations for principal military offences in all theatres in each year of the war. Executions are shown in brackets. Death sentences passed after the end of 1918 are not shown on this table.

Offence	1914	1915	1916	1917	1918
Desertion	16 (3)	241 (46)	528 (71)	760 (90)	445 (35)
Cowardice	20 (1)	51 (4)	79 (10)	43 (2)	20
Mutiny	0	1	11 (1)	2 (2)	7
Sleeping	39	238	115	41 (2)	16
Quitting	4	17 (2)	38 (2)	18 (2)	5 (1)
Disobedience	1	13 (1)	75* (3)	15 (1)	4
Casting away arms	0	1 (0)	3 (1)	2 (1)	0
Striking senior officer	0	10	24 (3)	8 (1)	7

* Includes 39 men of the Non-Combatant Corps.

Figure 5: Death Sentences Shown Annually (soldiers only[1])

Year	Death sentences	Monthly average
1914	85	17
1915	591	49
1916	856	71
1917	904	75
1918	515	43

Figure 6: Annual casualty totals for British Army[2]

Year	Casualties	Monthly average
1914	98, 689	19,738
1915	424,305	35,359
1916	700,513	58,376
1917	835,817	69,651
1918	890,922	80,993

Figure 7: Death sentences of 1914[3]

Offence	No. of death sentences	No. resulting in execution
Sleeping on post	39	0
Housebreaking	1	0
Desertion	16	3
Cowardice	20	1
Quitting post	4	0
Rape	1	0
AWOL	1	0
Offence against inhabitant	1	0
Disobedience	1	0
Drunk	1	0
Total	85	4

Figure 8: Death sentences in Irish regiments.
These are shown as percentage of British Army total (the number of executions of soldiers in Irish regiments is shown in brackets).

Year	Death sentences		Irish percentage
	Total	Irish	
1914	85	3	4
1915	591	59 (7)	10
1916	856	75 (7)	9
1917	904	59 (5)	6
1918	515	28 (3)	6
1919/1920	52	15 (3)	29
TOTAL	3,114	239 (25)	8

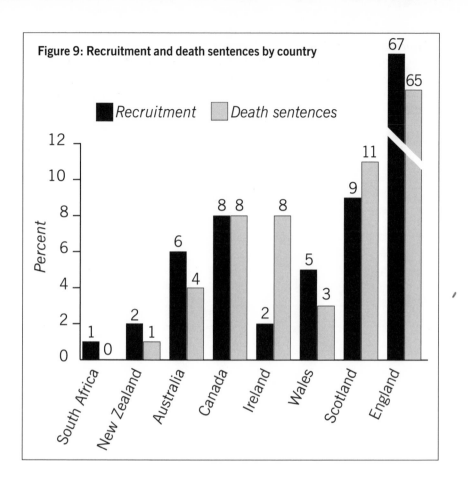

Figure 9: Recruitment and death sentences by country

Figure 10: Black units: death sentences and executions		
Regiment	Death sentences	Executed
British West Indies	8	4
Nigerian	2	1
Gold Coast	9	3
West Africa	1	1
Cape Coloured Labour Company	3	3

Figure 11: Death sentences confirmed by Commander-in-Chief ○/◡

Country	Death sentences	Executions	Percentage confirmed
England	1829	190	10
Scotland	310	38	12
Wales	91	13	14
Ireland	239	24	10
Australia	113	0	0
New Zealand	234	5	_22_
Canada	222	25	11
South Africa	11	1	9

Notes

Introduction

1 Anthony Babington, *For the Sake of Example*, Revised Edition (Barnsley, 1993), quotes the total number of executions as 346. Julian Putkowski and Julian Sykes, *Shot at Dawn*, revised edition (Barnsley, 1992), have traced 361 executions.

2 Gerard Oram, *Death Sentences passed by military courts of the British Army 1914–1924* (Francis Boutle, London, 1998).

3 War Office, *Statistics of the Military Effort of the British Empire During the Great War 1914–1920* (London, 1922) Part XXIII – Discipline.

4 Gerard Oram, *Death Sentences passed by military courts of the British Army 1914–1924* (London, 1998).

5 *Report of the Committee Convened by the Army Council to Enquire into the Law and Rules of Procedure Regulating Military Courts martial* – Darling Committee (HMSO, 1919).

6 Ernest Thurtle MP, *Shootings at Dawn. The Army Death Penalty at Work* (1924).

7 David Englander and James Osbourne, 'Jack, Tommy and Henry Dubb: The Armed Forces and the British Working Class' in *Historical Journal*, Volume 21 (London, 1978), argue that the target of Thurtle's attack was the army itself rather than the death penalty.

8 Babington, *For the Sake of Example*.

9 Putkowski & Sykes.

10 According to the 1920 War Office publication, *Soldiers Died in the Great War* (Polstead, Suffolk, 1988), the British Army suffered a daily average of 2,000 casualties, approximately 400 of whom were killed in action.

The British Army in 1914

1 Ian F. W. Beckett, 'The Military Historian and the Popular Image of the Western Front 1914–1918' in *The Historian*, No. 53 (Enfield, 1997), p. 12.

2 John M. Bourne, *Britain and the Great War 1914–1918* (London, 1989), p. 201.

3 Tim Travers, *The Killing Ground. The British Army and the Emergence of Modern Warfare, 1900–1918* (London, 1990), pp. 37–55.

4 Erskine Childers, *The Riddle of the Sands* (Harmondsworth, 1952), first published in 1903.

5 Ian V. Hogg, *The Guns 1914–18* (London, 1973), p. 22.

6 Travers, *The Killing Ground*, p. 94.

7 Travers, *The Killing Ground*, p.7.

8 Travers, *The Killing Ground*. Chapter one deals with the 'Edwardian Army'.

9 Travers, *The Killing Ground*, p. 109.

10 John Terraine, *The Great War* (Ware, 1997), p. xi.

11 On the 4 August 1914, Wilhelm II ordered his First Army to 'exterminate the treacherous England, walk over General French's contemptible little army.' Cited in Martin Gilbert, *First World War* (London 1994), p. 36. These first 100,000 British soldiers proudly adopted the nickname of 'the old contemptibles'.

12 Both Babington and Putkowski & Sykes have drawn a comparison with the lower numbers of executions in other armies.

13 Records of French courts martial are closed to the public for 100 years whereupon access to them will be reviewed.

14 Babington, *For the Sake of Example*, p. 118.

15 William Moore, *The Thin Yellow Line* (Barnsley, 1974), pp. 150–170.

16 Guy Pedroncini, *Les Mutineries de 1917* (Paris, 1967). Samuel Hynes, *A War Imagined* (London, 1990) cites Pedroncini's figures and states that the French executions totalled about the same as the British, 'or slightly fewer' (p. 214).

17 Pedroncini, pp. 3–9.

18 Leonard Smith, *Between Mutiny and Obedience: The Case of the French Fifth Infantry Division During World War One* (Princeton, 1994).

19 Hynes, p. 214.

20 Richard Evans, *Rituals of Retribution* (Oxford, 1996), p. 482.

21 Christoph Jahr, *Gewöhnliche Soldaten. Desertion und Deserteure im deutschen und britischen Heer 1914–1918*.(Vandenhoeck & Ruprecht, Göttingen, 1998)

22 Cited in Babington, *For the Sake of Example*, p. 191.

23 Moore, pp. 150–170.

24 Martin Stone, 'Shell-shock and the Psychologists' in W. F. Bynum (et al), *Anatomy of Madness*, volume II (London, 1985), pp. 242–271.

25 B. Holden Reid and J. White 'Desertion in the American Civil War' in L. Freedman (ed.) *War*, (Oxford, 1994), p. 139.

26 Holden Reid and White, p. 140.

27 Anthony Babington, *Shell-Shock: A History of the Changing Attitudes to War Neurosis* (Barnsley, 1997), pp. 13–20.

28 J. Galliher, G. Ray and B. Cook 'Abolition and Reinstatement of Capital Punishment in the Progressive Era and Early 20th Century' in *The Journal of Criminal Law and Criminology*, Volume 83, No. 3 (USA, 1992), pp. 538–578.

29 D. Englander, 'Mutinies and Military Morale' in Strachan, H. (ed.), *The Oxford Illustrated History of the First World War* (Oxford, 1998), pp. 191–203. I would like to thank Dr. Englander for access to this article prior to its publication.

30 Tim Travers, 'Technology, Tactics, and Morale: Jean de Bloch, the Boer War, and British Military Theory, 1900–1914' in *Journal of Modern History* 51 (June 1979), p. 286. He argues that the army should not be considered a separate institution but as a 'part of the conservative wing of public opinion in Edwardian Britain'.

31 Robert Graves, *Goodbye to All That* (Harmondsworth, 1960), p. 147.

32 Figures based on the comparative tables contained in Evans, pp. 934-935.

33 Cited in L. Radzinowicz and R. Hood, *A History of English Criminal Law*, Volume 5, *The Emergence of Penal Policy* (London, 1986), p. 672.

34 Cited in L. Radzinowicz and R. Hood, p. 673.

35 L. Radzinowicz and R. Hood, pp. 671–677. There are also the excellent comparative tables in R. Evans, *Rituals of Retribution*.

36 Evans, pp. 477–481.

37 Siegfried Sassoon, *The Complete Memoirs of George Sherston* (London, 1972), p. 342.

38 Captain Schweber MC, unpublished diary. Imperial War Museum ref. 86/65/1.

39 Brig. Gen. F. P. Crozier, *A Brass Hat in No Man's Land* (Bath, 1930), p. 204.

40 Cited in Putkowski & Sykes, p. 241.

41 Edwin Campion Vaughan, *Some Desperate Glory* (London, 1994), p. 225.

42 Babington, *For the Sake of Example*, pp. 12–13.

43 Gerald B. Hurst, 'The Administration of Military Law' in *Contemporary Review* (1919), p. 324.

44 Cited in Hurst, pp. 324-325.

45 Maxse papers. IWM 69/53/6.

46 PRO 213/7.

47 Darling Report, p. 8.

48 Darling Report, p. 8.

Sentenced to death

1 Siegfried Sassoon, *The Complete Memoirs of George Sherston*, (London, 1930), p. 257.

2 Rudyard Kipling, 'Epitaphs of the War (1914-1918) – The Coward' in *The Penguin Book of First World War Poetry* (Harmondsworth, 1981), p. 135.

3 War Office, *The Statistics of the Military Effort of the British Empire During the Great War 1914–1920.* (London, 1922).

4 Both Babington, *For the Sake of Example*, and Putkowski & Sykes, quote this figure in their introductions.

5 PRO ref. WO213/1–WO213/34 inclusive.

6 G. Oram, *Death Sentences.*

7 PRO WO93/51.

8 See the comparative table in G. Oram, *Death Sentences*, p. 15.

9 G. Oram, *Death Sentences*, p. 15.

10 Julian Putkowski has been researching mutinies in the British Army and has found that the official statistics underestimate the numbers convicted and the true number is closer to 2,000. See J. Putkowski, *British Army Mutineers 1914–1922* (Francis Boutle Publishers, London, 1998).

11 War Office, *Statistics of the Military Effort of the British Empire During the Great War 1914–1920.*

12 Major T. J. Mitchell and Miss G. M. Smith, *History of the Great War Based on Official Documents – Medical Services: Casualties and Medical Statistics of the Great War* (London, 1931), p. 7.

13 *Statistics of the Military Effort of the British Empire During the Great War 1914–1920* (War Office, 1922).

14 Mitchell and Smith, *Medical Services*, p. 7.

15 Source: *Statistics of the Military Effort.*

16 Putkowski and Sykes, pp. 292–298.

17 This information comes from Julian Putkowski who informs me that the original methodology was flawed. The new edition of *Shot at Dawn*, due in 1999, is eagerly awaited.

18 PRO WO213/2.

19 PRO WO71/387.

20 PRO WO71/388.

21 PRO WO213/2.

22 PRO WO71/389.

23 PRO WO71/390.

24 Details of all these cases can be found in G. Oram, *Death Sentences.*

25 PRO WO213/3.

26 Oram, *Death Sentences.*

27 PRO WO213/3.

28 PRO WO71/393.

29 PRO WO213/3.

30 PRO WO213/3.

31 PRO WO71/525

32 PRO WO71/526.
33 PRO WO256/10.
34 Travers, *The Killing Ground*, p. 146.
35 PRO WO213/13 – 31 inc. for overseas figures.
   PRO WO86/75 – 79 inc. & PRO WO92/3 – 4 inc.
   for home figures.
36 PRO WO 71/631 & PRO WO71/632.
37 PRO WO71/599.
38 PRO WO71/600.
39 Brig. E. A. James, *British Regiments, 1914–18*,
   4th edition, (London, 1993).
40 Average ration strength, that is the total number
   of rations provided for each month of the year
   divided by twelve.
41 Includes killed, wounded, missing and taken
   prisoner. Some wounded were returned to the
   front, therefore it is possible that men were
   occasionally counted twice.
42 Includes those lost temporarily or permanently
   because of illness or disease. Again some may
   have been counted more than once, which
   explains why in 1915 the total number of
   casualties exceeded the average ration strength.
43 Mitchell & Smith, *Medical Services*.
44 This figure excludes the thirty-nine conscientious
   objectors of the Non-Combatant Corps who were
   sentenced to death for disobedience on the
   Western Front in June 1916. Inclusion of these
   cases would distort the true figure. There is some
   ambiguity concerning the actual number of these
   cases: John Stevenson, *British Society 1914–45*
   (Harmondsworth, 1991), cites the number as
   forty-one (p. 64), while Arthur Marwick, *The
   Deluge* (London, 1991), states that the number
   of conscientious objectors sentenced to death
   was thirty-four (p. 121). The courts martial
   registers – PRO WO 213/9-10 inc. – record
   details of thirty-nine such cases, five were not
   confirmed thereby supporting Marwick's figures.
   All the death sentences were commuted to ten
   years penal servitude with the exception of four,
   which were not confirmed.
45 One of the eleven death sentences for mutiny was
   not confirmed, indicating that it was not a
   satisfactory conviction. A fourth execution for
   mutiny on the Western Front was carried out on
   an Egyptian labourer, Mohammed Ahmed. Again
   this has been omitted from the figures, which
   have been restricted to soldiers, to avoid
   distortion
46 Another death sentence for mutiny was passed in
   1919 but not implemented.
47 PRO WO71/535.
48 Private Aziberi Frafra of the Gold Coast Regiment
   was sentenced to death on 19th September
   1916 and executed just nine days later. PRO
   WO71/538.
49 Mitchell & Smith, p. 198.
50 The *Official History* records a mere 304 British
   officers and men as taken prisoner during the
   entire Dardanelles campaign. Mitchell and
   Smith, p. 202.
51 Mitchell & Smith, p. 187.
52 Mitchell & Smith, p. 222.
53 Mitchell & Smith, pp. 217–245.
54 Privates Burton and Downing of the South
   Lancashire Regiment were both shot in 1917 for
   sleeping at their posts and became the only such
   cases in the British Army. PRO WO90/7,
   WO71/631 & WO71/632.
55 Mitchell & Smith, pp. 176–185.
56 Ernst Jünger, *The Storm of Steel* (London,
   1994).
57 It would be incorrect to refer to different nations
   within the British Isles, not even for the Irish.
   Instead, the word country is preferred as
   England, Scotland, Wales and Ireland were
   readily identifiable parts of Britain.
58 *Statistics of the Military Effort*.
59 A very good discussion of recruitment during
   World War One is Peter Simkins, 'The Four
   Armies 1914–1918' in David Chandler and Ian
   Beckett (eds), *The Oxford History of the British
   Army* (Oxford, 1996), pp. 235–255.
60 James, *British Regiments*.
61 *Soldiers Died in the Great War*.
62 Two officers were executed for desertion (these
   are dealt with in a later chapter) and the other
   two had their sentences commuted. A further
   officer was sentenced to death after the war and
   another was executed for murder.

The Irish question

1 Terence Denman, 'The Catholic Irish Soldier in
   the First World War' in *Irish Historical Studies*,
   Volume 27 (November 1991), pp. 352–365,
   states that in 1830 the Irish made up 42 per cent
   of the British Army.
2 Keith Jeffrey, 'The Post-War Army' in I. F. W.
   Beckett and K. Simpson (eds) *A Nation in Arms*
   (Manchester, 1985), p. 219.
3 Terence Denman, 'Ethnic Soldiers Pure and
   Simple? The Irish in the Late Victorian Army' in
   War in History, Volume 3, Number 3 (1996), p.
   253.
4 The six 'Irish' battalions raised in Tyneside were
   equivalent to one and a half infantry brigades.
5 Private James Wilson of the 4th battalion
   Canadian Expeditionary Force was executed on
   9th July 1916. He had previously served with the
   Connaught Rangers. PRO WO71/489.
6 James, *British Regiments*, gives the location
   where each New Army battalion was formed. The
   information cited above is based on a composite
   of all the Irish regiments.
7 *Report on Recruiting in Ireland*, (HMSO, 1916),

8 *Report on Recruiting in Ireland*, p. 3.
9 *Statistics of the Military Effort*, p. 363.
10 A. T. Q. Stewart, *The Ulster Crisis: Resistance to Home Rule 1912–1914* (Belfast, 1997), p. 226.
11 This was one third of the entire infantry strength. No doubt concerns over a possible invasion also played a part in this decision.
12 *Statistics of the Military Effort*, p. 363.
13 Numbers of battle honours and Victoria crosses are listed in James, *British Regiments*, Appendix VII, pp. 135–137.
14 Major Edward Mannock VC was Irish and a Nationalist. He was also a fighter 'ace' who fought with 'conspicuous valour'. J. M. Bourne, p. 213.
15 Hugh A. MacDougall, *Racial Myth in English History: Trojans, Teutons and Anglo-Saxons* (Montreal, 1982).
16 See Mary Hickman, *Religion, Class and Identity*, (Aldershot, 1995).
17 Charles Kingsley, *The Water Babies*, (Harmondsworth, 1995).
18 Kingsley, p. 233.
19 Hickman.
20 Hickman, p. 54.
21 Stone, 'Shell-shock and the Psychologists'.
22 *The Times*, 8 April 1915.
23 Captain J. C. Dunn, a Medical Officer with the Royal Welsh Fusiliers, claimed that the Jews and the Irish were poor soldiers.
24 Ted Bogacz, 'War Neurosis and Cultural Change in England, 1914 – 1922: The Work of the War Office Committee of Enquiry into shell-shock,' in *Journal of Contemporary History*, volume 24 (London, 1989), p 249.
25 *Report of the Committee of Enquiry into Shell-shock* (HMSO, 1922), p. 96.
26 PRO WO32/4747, minutes 12A and 13A.
27 Katherine Castle, *Britannia's Children – Reading Colonialism Through Children's Books and Magazines* (Manchester, 1996).
28 Alan Clark, *The Donkeys* (London, 1991), p. 27.
29 David R. Woodward, 'introduction' in D. R. Woodward (ed.), *The Military Correspondence of Field-Marshal Sir William Robertson, Chief of the Imperial Genera Staff, December 1915 – February 1918* (London, 1989).
30 Robert Blake (ed.), *The Private Papers of Douglas Haig 1914–1919* (London, 1952), p. 114.
31 Blake, p. 123.
32 Blake, p. 296.
33 Blake, p. 296.
34 Denman, *Ethnic Soldiers*, p. 263.
35 Trevor Wilson, *The Myriad Faces of War* (Cambridge, 1986), p. 51.
36 Joseph Keating, 'The Tyneside Irish Brigade' in

Felix Lavery (ed.), *Great Irishmen in War and Politics* (London, 1920).
37 Wilson, p. 68.
38 As well as many 'Macs' and 'O's' tried by courts martial after the rebellion there are others such as Pearse, Davys, Williams and Wilson to name but a few, although some of these names might have been anglicised. For example, Collins is the anglicised form of O'Coileáin.
39 Gloden Dallas & Douglas Gill, *The Unknown Army* (London, 1985), p. 48.
40 Cited in Denman, *Catholic Irish Soldier*, p. 358.
41 Bourne, p. 214.
42 Blake, p. 299.
43 Sassoon, p. 309.
44 PRO WO213/2.
45 PRO WO213/3.
46 PRO WO71/394.
47 PRO WO71/394.
48 Out of thirteen battalions from the various Regiments of Guards that saw active service in the war only two were Irish. One Coldstream Guardsman and a Scots Guardsman were executed as well as the three Irish Guardsmen.
49 PRO WO71/401.
50 PRO WO71/402.
51 PRO WO71/431.
52 Private Fatoma, West African Regiment, was executed on 19 July 1915. PRO WO71/429.
53 PRO WO71/659.
54 PRO 92/4.
55 Christoph Jahr, *Gewöhnliche Soldaten. Desertion und Deserteure im deutschen und britischen Heer 1914-1918*. (Vandenhoeck & Ruprecht, Göttingen, 1998)
56 James Joll, *1914 – The Unspoken Assumptions* (London, 1968).

The imperial crisis

1 Travers, *The Killing Ground*, p. 5.
2 Travers, *The Killing Ground*, p. 13.
3 G. R. Searle, *Eugenics and Politics in Britain 1900–1914* (Leyden, 1976).
4 J. M. Winter, 'Military Fitness and Civilian Health in Britain During the First World War' in *Journal of Contemporary History*, volume 15 (London 1980), pp. 211–244.
5 G. R. Searle, p. 23.
6 *Memorandum of the Director-General, Army Medical Service, on the Physical Unfitness of Men Offering Themselves for Enlistment in the Army*, (HMSO, 1903), p. 3. Hereafter referred to as 'Memorandum of D.G., Army Medical Service'.
7 *Memorandum of D.G., Army Medical Service*, p. 3.
8 *Memorandum of the D. G., Army Medical Service*, p. 6.
9 H. G. Wells, 'The Land Ironclads (1903)' in

Selected Short Stories (Harmondsworth, 1958), p. 105.

10 H. G. Wells, 'The Land Ironclads', p. 105.

11 *Memorandum of the D. G., Army Medical Service*, p. 7.

12 Daniel Pick, *Faces of Degeneration* (Cambridge, 1989). In 1909 C.F.G. Masterman was writing of the urban masses in such terms.

13 D. Pick, *Degeneration*,. p.202

14 Evidence presented to the Royal Commission in 1908 by Sir Clifford Allbutt, the Regius Professor of Physics at Cambridge, cited in Radzinowicz and Hood, pp. 318-319.

15 Cited in D. Pick, *Faces of Degeneration*, p. 192.

16 W. A. Potts, 'Causation of Mental Defect in Children' in *British Medical Journal*, Vol. 2 (1905).

17 G. R. Searle, p. 93.

18 G. R. Searle, p. 93.

19 G. R. Searle, p. 110.

20 Cited in G. R. Searle, p. 93.

21 G. R. Searle, pp. 95–105.

22 G. R. Searle, p. 104.

23 Cited in Radzinowicz and Hood, pp. 316–317.

24 Cited in Radzinowicz and Hood, p. 321.

25 Radzinowicz and Hood, p. 323.

26 Radzinowicz and Hood, p. 317.

27 Anders Adolf Retzius, 'A Glance at the Present State of Ethnology with Reference to the Form of the Skull', (English translation) in the *British and Foreign Medico-Chiururgical Review* (25), 1860, pp. 366 ff.

28 Sir Arthur Conan Doyle, *The Lost World and Other Stories* (Ware, 1995), p. 20.

29 Daniel Pick, *Faces of Degeneration*, p. 165.

30 Radzinowicz & Hood, p.326.

31 Radzinowicz & Hood, p.327.

32 Cited in G. R. Searle, p. 107.

33 Cited in G. R. Searle, p. 108.

34 Cited in Radzinowicz and Hood, p. 334.

35 Cited in Radzinowicz & Hood, p.335.

36 Pick, *Degeneration*, p. 177.

37 Bogacz, p. 255. Dunn served in the same unit as Sassoon and appears in the 1926 poem 'A Footnote on the War'.

38 Keith Surridge, 'All you soldiers are what we call pro-Boer': The Military Critique of the South African War, 1899–1902' in *History* (October, 1997) p. 600.

39 See Daniel Pick, *War Machine*. In particular pp. 88–114. The Franco-Prussian War was viewed, by some, as the ultimate test of Teuton versus Gaul or, to put it more specifically into British parlance, Saxon versus Celt.

40 Pick, *War Machine* (London, 1993), p.173.

41 Colonel C. H. Melville, *Eugenics and Military Service*, contained in, *Eugenics Review 1910–1911*, p. 53. The author's rank of Colonel

was equivalent to that of a battalion commander in the field with command of approximately 1,000 men.

42 Melville, p. 54.

43 Cited in M. Brown, *The Imperial War Museum Book of the Western Front*, p. 268.

44 Winter, 'Military Fitness', p. 217.

45 Travers, *The Killing Ground*, p. 146.

46 Cited in Travers, *The Killing Ground*, p. 51.

47 J. M. Winter, 'Military Fitness', p.215.

48 Lord Moran, *The Anatomy of Courage*, 2nd edition (London, 1965), p. 151.

49 Moran, p. 151.

50 Jon Stallworthy (ed.), *The Poems of Wilfred Owen* (London, 1990), p.151.

51 J. M. Winter, 'Britain's Lost Generation of the First World War' in *Population Studies*, Volume 31, No. 3 (London, 1977), pp. 449–466.

52 Desmond Morton, *When Your Number's Up: The Canadian Soldier in the First World War* (Toronto, 1993), p. 251.

53 Cited in D. Pick, *Faces of Degeneration*, p. 228.

The worthless men

1 PRO WO71/405.

2 Ernst Jünger, *The Storm of Steel*, p. 158.

3 Lord Moran, *The Anatomy of Courage*, 2nd edition (London, 1966), p. 151.

4 Travers, *The Killing Ground* p.37.

5 Stone, p. 248.

6 Babington, *Shell-shock*, p. 43. See also C. S. Myers, *Shell-shock in France* (Cambridge, 1940).

7 The work of Sir John Collie, an insurance fraud doctor before the war, is of particular importance in this respect. See Peter J. Leese, *A Social and Cultural History of Shell-shock, with Particular Reference to the Experience of British Soldiers During and After the Great War*, unpublished PhD thesis, Open University, 1989.

8 Stone, p.255.

9 The case of Private Hopkins, Lancashire Fusiliers, who was executed on 13th February 1918. PRO WO71/635.

10 John Buchan, *The Complete Richard Hannay* (Harmondsworth, 1992), p. 256.

11 Hickman, p. 50.

12 Melville, p. 53.

13 Travers, *The Killing Ground*, p. 39.

14 Cited in Hynes,, p. 225. Raymond Asquith, the Prime Minister's son, was a barrister by profession. He enlisted in the Grenadier Guards and was killed during the Battle of the Somme. He is buried at Guillemont Road Cemetery in France.

15 Arthur Conan-Doyle, *The Lost World* (Ware, 1995), p. 109.

16 W. H. R. Rivers, *Instinct and the Unconscious*

(1922).

17 Dr. D. Forsyth, 'Functional Nerve Disease and Shock of Battle' in *The Lancet* (December, 1915), p. 1399.

18 Forsyth, 'Functional Nerve Disease and Shock of Battle', p. 1399.

19 Stone, p.252.

20 Stone, *Shell-shock and the Psychologists*, p.245.

21 According to Stone, Myers had coined the term 'shell-shock' in early 1915, p. 257. By 1916 the term was in widespread use amongst senior army officers and medical officers when reviewing courts martial cases.

22 Stone, p. 253.

23 Stone, p. 250.

24 The view was expressed by Mary Dendy, a member of the Eugenics Education Society from 1905. Although explicitly aimed at 'fallen' women the universal acceptance of the association is relevant to our discussion. See Radzinowicz and Hood, p. 328.

25 Forsyth, 'Functional Nerve Disease and Shock of Battle', p. 1399.

26 Forsyth, 'Functional Nerve Disease and Shock of Battle', p. 1399.

27 See Radzinowicz and Hood, p. 321.

28 PRO WO71/537.

29 For accounts of treatment of shell-shock cases see Eric Leed, *No Man's Land* and Peter Leese, *A Social and Cultural History of Shell-shock*.

30 For the best account of the impact of the war on psychology and psychiatric practice in Britain see Martin Stone's excellent essay 'Shell-shock and the Psychologists'.

31 Stone, p. 255.

32 Stone, p. 256.

33 Stone, p. 250.

34 Bogacz, p. 249.

35 *Report of the War Office Committee of Enquiry into Shell-shock* (HMSO, 1922), p. 46. Hereafter referred to as the '*Southborough Report*'.

36 *Southborough Report*, p. 16.

37 *Southborough Report*, p. 64.

38 Ernst Jünger, *The Storm of Steel*, p. 4.

39 *Southborough Report*, p. 28.

40 Bogacz, p. 249.

41 *SouthboroughReport*, p. 95.

42 *Southborough Report*, p. 96.

43 PRO WO71/405.

44 PRO WO71/405.

45 PRO WO71/405.

46 PRO WO71/422.

47 PRO WO71/406.

48 PRO WO71/406.

49 PRO WO71/412.

50 PRO WO71/416.

51 PRO WO71/414.

52 PRO WO71/423.

53 Twenty-one was the age of majority at the time of the war. At least thirty-two twenty-year-olds, fourteen nineteen-year-olds, three eighteen-year-olds, two seventeen-year-olds and one sixteen-year-old were executed by British firing squads. It has proved impossible to obtain an age in every single case, therefore these figures are likely to be higher.

54 PRO WO71/404.

55 PRO WO93/49.

56 PRO WO71/441.

57 Cited in Lyn McDonald, *1915; The Death of Innocence*, (London, 1993), p. 327.

58 Clive Hughes, 'The New Armies' in Beckett, I. F. W. and Simpson, K., *A Nation in Arms*, p. 112.

59 General Haig often preached the usefulness of 'trench-raiding' because it prevented his troops from becoming idle and kept them in a state of war-readiness. The truth was that trench raids were, in terms of manpower, an extremely expensive activity usually costing many lives for very little return. Often the intelligence gathered, at great cost, from such raids was not acted upon as it should have been. An example of this is the intelligence gathered from prisoners before the first German gas attack which indicated that the Germans were moving large canisters of gas with fitted valves up to the front line. The attack, when it came, took the front line troops by surprise causing widespread panic. If the Germans had realised this a rout could easily have ensued.

60 PRO WO71/535.

61 PRO WO71/534.

62 PRO WO71/534.

63 PRO WO71/534.

64 PRO WO71/534.

65 PRO WO71/534.

66 Cited in Putkowski & Sykes, pp. 157-158.

67 G. Oram, *Death Sentences*.

68 H. M. Davson, *The History of the 35th Division* (London, 1926).

69 PRO WO213/13.

70 Thurtle, p. 7. Putkowski & Sykes state that the 'little girl' must have been the daughter of Lance-Corporal McDonald, for the other two had no children.

71 PRO WO71/635.

72 PRO WO71/635.

73 PRO WO71/635.

74 PRO WO71/635.

75 PRO WO71/635.

76 PRO WO71/488.

77 I am indebted to Private Nelson's niece, Mrs. Nora High, for the information concerning his family background.

78 PRO WO71/467.

79 Thurtle, *Shootings at Dawn*.
80 Putkowski & Sykes, p. 68.
81 PRO WO71/450.
82 PRO WO71/450.
83 PRO WO71/456.
84 Putkowski & Sykes, p. 236.
85 PRO WO71/677.
86 PRO WO71/677.
87 PRO WO71/677.
88 PRO WO71/677.
89 PRO WO71/661.
90 PRO WO71/661.
91 A third officer, Second-Lieutenant John Patterson of the Essex Regiment, was executed for murdering a Military Police Sergeant who attempted to arrest Patterson for cashing forged cheques. Patterson was shot for his crime on the 24th September 1918.
92 PRO WO71/1027.
93 PRO WO71/1027.
94 PRO WO71/1027.
95 PRO WO71/1027.
96 PRO WO71/1027.
97 PRO WO71/1027.
98 PRO WO71/1027.
99 PRO WO71/1027.
100 PRO WO71/1027.
100 Babington, *For the Sake of Example*, p. 102.
102 Babington, *For the Sake of Example*, p. 103.
103 Unpublished diary of T. MacMillan, Imperial War Museum, pp. 169-170.
104 Three Lieutenants had their death sentences commuted but two Second-Lieutenants (one was for murder and therefore need not concern us here) and a Sub-Lieutenant had their sentences confirmed.

In black and white

1 The title of a collection of stories by Rudyard Kipling (published 1888) purporting to give a voice to the Indian characters. According to Salman Rushdie they remain 'a testament to the old quarrel of colonizer and colonized' [sic]. R. Kipling, *Soldiers Three and In Black and White* (Harmondsworth, 1993) p. xv.
2 D. Killingray, 'Race and Rank in the British Army in the Twentieth Century' in *Ethnic and Racial Studies*, Volume 10, Number 3 (July, 1987).
3 Rudyard Kipling, *In Black and White*, p. 110.
4 Rudyard Kipling, *In Black and White*, pp. 168–169.
5 Salman Rushdie, 'Introduction' in Rudyard Kipling, *In Black and White*, p. xiv.
6 Thomas R. Metcalf, *Ideologies of the Raj*, (Cambridge, 1997), p. 111.
7 Metcalf, p. 163.
8 Castle, pp. 12–28.
9 Castle, p. 15.
10 Metcalf, p. 127.
11 In fact more Indians were recruited than Scots, Welsh and Irish added together. Only in England were more soldiers recruited than in India.
12 The Indian memorial at Neuve Chapelle is one of the most impressive Commonwealth memorials in France. Its Indian-style architecture makes it very conspicuous, which may explain why it was treated so badly during the Nazi occupation.
13 Metcalf, p. 163.
14 Blake, p. 78.
15 L. James, *Mutiny* (London, 1987), p. 221. Under interrogation one mutineer had apparently confessed that one of the subjects of the sermons in the Mosque on Fridays had been the 'unholy' nature of this war. Indeed, in 1918 the Turkish commander, Enver Pasha, declared a *jihad* which caused the War Office to think in terms of defending India only with white troops. (James, p. 216).
16 Gilbert, p. 131.
17 Unpublished diary of A. H. Dickinson. Imperial War Museum.
18 Martin Gilbert also wrongly identifies a photograph of Indian soldiers in a trench on the Western Front as being Sikh (opposite p. 168 of his book *First World War*) when their turbans are clearly not tied in the Sikh manner. They are in fact Baluchis.
19 Unpublished diary of Lieutenant Gell, Imperial War Museum.
20 Malcolm Brown, *The Imperial War Museum of the Western Front* (London, 1993), p. 98.
21 Brown, p.98.
22 PRO WO90/7.
23 PRO WO71/629.
24 PRO WO71/675.
25 PRO WO71/595.
26 PRO WO71/594.
27 PRO WO71/576.
28 G. Oram, *Death Sentences*.
29 PRO WO71/538.
30 PRO WO71/575.
31 PRO WO71/674.
32 G. Oram, *Death Sentences*.
33 PRO WO71/429.
34 Cited in Putkowski & Sykes, p. 264.
35 PRO WO71/676.
36 PRO WO71/688.
37 PRO WO71/600.
38 There is some confusion over the actual offence with which Mohamed Ahmed was convicted. Some sources, including Putkowski & Sykes, state that it was for mutiny. However the courts martial register PRO WO213/17 records the offence as 'violence'.
39 PRO WO213/34. In 1919, eleven members of the so-called Slavo-British Penal Battalion were

shot for mutiny, seven other mutineers along with one convicted of sedition and another of going absent without leave had their death sentences commuted. The following year, five Macedonian Muleteers were also executed for murder. PRO WO213/34.

40 PRO WO71/684 & 685.

41 PRO WO71/686.

42 David Englander, 'Manpower in the British Army 1914–1918' in Gerard Canini (ed.) *Les Fronts Invisibles* (Nancy, France, 1984), p. 102.

43 PRO WO213/9.

44 PRO WO213/3.

45 John Buchan, *The Complete Richard Hannay* (Harmondsworth, 1992), p. 215.

46 John Buchan, p. 239.

47 Siegfried Sassoon, *The Complete Memoirs of George Sherston*, p. 342.

48 Ernst Jünger, *The Storm of Steel* (London, 1994), p. 154.

49 Jünger, p. 262.

50 Corporal A. Wickens, 9 Rifle Brigade, who was executed on 7th March 1918 for the murder of a prostitute. PRO WO71/636.

The final judgement

1 Travers, *The Killing Ground*, pp. 86–89.

2 Travers, *The Killing Ground*, p. 106.

3 Blake, p. 290. See also Babington, *For the Sake of Example*, p. 191.

4 Not including labourers who were to all intents and purposes 'in the army'.

5 Blake, p. 290.

6 Blake, p. 291.

7 Blake, p. 313.

8 Morton, *When Your Number's Up*, p. 251.

Notes to the Appendix

1 Figure does not include the 39 men of the Non-Combatant Corps sentenced to death in 1916 but does include men of the Labour Corps.

2 Source: *Statistics of the Military Effort of the British Empire During the Great War 1914–1920* (War Office, 1922).

3 Source PRO WO213/1-3 inclusive.

4 C Pugsley, *On the Fringe of Hell* (Auckland, 1991), pp. 350–351, identifies four more commuted death sentences from sources in New Zealand. Inclusion of these cases would reduce the confirmation rate to nineteen per cent, which is still much higher than for soldiers from other countries.

Bibliography

Primary Sources – Unpublished:

Public Record Office Files:
CAB17/34: Correspondence
   concerning Channel-Tunnel.
HO139/9/32: MI 5 Correspondence.
WO32/4747: Minutes of the
   Committee of Enquiry into Shell-
   Shock.
WO71/387 – WO71/1238 inclusive:
   Judge Advocate General's
   recordsCourts martial.
WO90/6 – WO/90/8 inclusive: Register
   of General Courts martial (abroad).
WO92/3 & WO92/4: Register of
   General Courts martial (home).
WO93/49 – WO93/51 inclusive: Judge
   Advocate General's Office statistics.
WO213/1 – WO213/34 inclusive:
   Register of Field General Courts
   martial.

Imperial War Museum Records:
Dickinson A. H. – Diary.
Gell, Lieutenant – Diary.
MacMillan T. – Diary.
Maxse Papers
Schweber, Captain, MC – Diary, ref.
   86/65/1.
Unidentified Soldier – Diary, ref. Misc.
   550.

Primary Sources – Published:
*Government Publications, Registers,
Official Reports and Histories*
Davson, H. M., The History of the 35th
   Division (London, 1926).
*Documents Relative to the Sinn Fein
   Movement* (London, 1921).
Imperial War Graves Commission,
   Register of War Cemeteries.
Memorandum by the Director-General,
   Army Medical Service, on the
   Physical Unfitness of Men Offering
   Themselves for Enlistment in the
   Army (HMSO, 1903).
Memorandum on the Censorship
   (HMSO, 1915).
Mitchell, T. J. and Smith, G. M.,
   *Official History of the Great War –
   Medical Services* (London, 1931).
Report on Recruiting in Ireland (HMSO,
   1916).
Report of the Committee Constituted by
   the Army Council to Enquire into the
   Law and Rules of Procedure
   Regulating Military Courts martial –
   Darling Committee (HMSO, 1919).
Report of the War Office Committee of
   Enquiry into Shell-Shock –
   Southborough Committee (HMSO,
   1922).
War Office, *Manual of Military Law*
   (London, 1914).
War Office, *Statistics of the Military
   Effort of the British Empire in the
   Great War 1914 – 1920* (London,
   1922).
War Office, *Soldiers Died in the Great
   War*, Volumes 1 – 80 inclusive
   (London, 1920).

*Newspapers, Journals and other
Articles*
Catholic Bulletin (Dublin, 1917).
Conway, M., *The Crowd in Peace and*

War (London, 1915).

Fifth Glo'ster Gazette 1915-1919 (Stroud, 1993).

Forsyth, D., 'Functional Nerve Disease and Shock of Battle' in *The Lancet,* 25th December 1915.

Hurst, G. B., 'The Administration of Military Law' in *Contemporary Review* (1919).

Maudsley, H., 'War Psychology: English and German' in *Journal of Medical Science* (1919).

Melville, C. H., 'Eugenics and Military Service' in *Eugenics Review,* 1910–1911.

Montague, C. E., *Disenchantment* (London, 1924).

Myers, C., *Shell-shock in France* (London, 1940).

Retzius, A. A., 'A Glance at the Present State of Ethnology to the Form of the Skull' (English translation) in *British and Foreign Medico-Chirurgical Review*, No. 25 (1860).

Rivers, W. H. R., *Instinct and the Unconscious* (London, 1922).

Sinn Fein Rebellion Handbook: Easter 1916 (Dublin, 1917).

Thurtle, E., *Shootings at Dawn* (London, 1922).

The Times.

Wells, H. G., 'Why Britain Went to War' in *The War Illustrated*, 22 August 1914.

Wells, H. G., 'The War Twenty Years After' in Hammerton, J. A., *World War* (London, 1930).

Diaries, Letters and Memoirs

Blake, R. (ed.), *The Private Papers of Douglas Haig* (London, 1952).

Crozier, F. P., *A Brass Hat in No Man's Land* (London, 1930).

Crozier, F. P., The Men I Killed (London, 1937).

Dunn, J. C., *The War the Infantry Knew* (London, 1987).

Gurney, I., *War Letters* (London, 1984).

Graves, R., *Goodbye to All That* (Harmondsworth, 1960).

Jünger, E., *The Storm of Steel* (London, 1994).

Ludendorff, E., *My War Memories 1914–1918* (London, 1929).

Myers, C. S., *Shell-shock in France* (Cambridge, 1940).

Owen, H. and Bell J., *Collected Letters of Wilfred Owen* (Oxford, 1967).

Vaughan, E. C., *Some Desperate Glory* (London, 1994).

Woodward, D. R. (ed.), *The Military Correspondence of Field-Marshal Sir William Robertson, Chief of the Imperial General Staff December 1915–February 1918* (London, 1989).

Poetry and Fiction

Buchan, J., *The Complete Richard Hannay* (Harmondsworth, 1992).

Childers, E., *The Riddle of the Sands* (Harmondsworth, 1952).

Doyle, A. C., T*he Lost World and Other Stories* (Ware, 1995).

Glover, J. and Silkin J. (eds), *First World War Prose* (Harmondsworth, 1990).

Gurney, I., *Severn & Somme and War's Embers* (Northumberland, 1997).

Herbert, A. P., *The Secret Battle* (London, 1936).

Kingsley, C., *The Water Babies* (Harmondsworth, 1995).

Kipling, R., *Soldiers Three and In Black and White* (Harmondsworth, 1993).

Montague, C. E., *Rough Justice* (London, 1941).

Sassoon, S., *The Complete Memoirs of George Sherston* (London, 1930).

Sassoon, S., *The War Poems* (London, 1983).

Stallworthy, J. (ed.), *The Poems of*

Wilfred Owen (London, 1990).

Wells, H. G., *Selected Short Stories* (Harmondsworth, 1958).

Secondary Sources:

Adams, R. J. Q. and Poirier, P. P., *The Conscription Controversy in Great Britain 1900–1918* (London, 1987).

Babington, A., *For the Sake of Example* (Barnsley, 1993).

Babington, A., *Shell-Shock: a History of the Changing Attitudes to War Neurosis* (Barnsley, 1997).

Baynes, J., *Morale: A Study of Men and Courage. The Second Scottish Rifles at the Battle of Neuve Chapelle 1915* (London, 1967).

Becker, J. J., *The Great War and the French People* (Leamington Spa, 1985).

Beckett, I. F. W., 'Total War' in Emsley, C., Marwick, A. and Simpson, W., *War, Peace and Social Change in Twentieth-Century Europe* (Milton Keynes 1989).

Beckett, I. F. W. and Simpson, K. (eds), *A Nation in Arms. A Social Study of The British Army in the First World War* (Manchester, 1985).

Bessel, R. and Englander, D., 'Up From the Trenches: Some Recent Writings on Soldiers of the Great War' in *European Studies Review* Volume 11 (London, 1981).

Best, G., 'Militarism and the Victorian Public School' in Simon, B. and Bradley, I. (eds), *The Victorian Public School* (Dublin, 1975).

Best, G., *Humanity in Warfare* (London, 1980).

Bogacz, T., 'War Neurosis and Cultural Change in England, 1914-22: The Work of The War Office Committee of Enquiry into shell-shock, *Journal of Contemporary History* Vol. 24 (London, 1989).

Bond, B., *War and Society in Europe 1870–1970* (Stroud, 1998).

Bourne, J. M., *Britain and the Great War 1914–1918* (London, 1991).

Brown, M., *The Imperial War Museum Book of the Western Front* (London, 1993).

Bushaway, B., 'Name Upon Name: The Great War and Remembrance' in Porter, R. (ed.), *Myths of the English* (Cambridge 1993).

Bynum, W. F., Porter, R. and Shepherd, M., *Anatomy of Madness*, Volume II (London, 1985).

Castle, K., *Britannia's Children; Reading Colonialism Through Children's Books and Magazines* (Manchester, 1996).

Chandler, D. and Beckett, I. F. W., *The Oxford History of the British Army* (Oxford, 1996).

Clark, A., *The Donkeys* (London, 1991).

Dallas, G. and Gill, D., *The Unknown Army* (London, 1985).

Dangerfield, G., *The Strange Death of Liberal England* (London, 1936).

De Groot, G., 'Educated Soldier or Cavalry Officer? Contradictions in the pre–1914 Career of Douglas Haig' in *War and Society*, Vol. 4, No. 2 (Sept. 1986).

Denman, T., 'The Catholic Irish Soldier in the First World War: The 'Racial Environment' in *Irish Historical Studies*, Vol. 17, No. 108 (Nov. 1991).

Denman, T., 'Ethnic Soldiers Pure and Simple'? The Irish in the Late Victorian British Army' in *War in History*, Vol. 3, No. 3 (1996).

Dixon, N., *On the Psychology of Military Incompetence* (London, 1979).

Edmonds, J. E., *A Short History of World War I* (London, 1951).

Englander, D., 'Military Intelligence and

the Defence of the Realm: The Surveillance of Civilians and Soldiers During the First World War' in *Bulletin for the Study of Labour History*, Volume 52, Number 1 (London, 1987).

Englander, D. and Osbourne, J., 'Jack, Tommy and Henry Dubb: the Armed Forces and the British Working class' in *Historical Journal,* Volume 21 (London, 1978).

Englander, D., 'Manpower in the British Army, 1914-1918' in Canini, G., *Les Fronts Invisibles* (Nancy, 1984).

Englander, D., 'Soldiering and Identity: Reflections on the Great War' in *War in History* 1994 1 (3), pp. 300-318.

Englander, D., 'Mutinies and Military Morale' in Strachan, H. (ed.), *The Oxford Illustrated History of the First World War* (Oxford, 1998).

Evans, R. J., *Rituals of Retribution, Capital Punishment in Germany 1600–1987* (Oxford, 1996).

Foster, R. F., *Modern Ireland 1600–1972* (Harmondsworth, 1989).

Foster, R. F., *Paddy and Mr. Punch: Connections in Irish and English History* (Harmondsworth, 1993).

Freedman, L., (ed.) *War* (Oxford, 1994).

Fuller, J. G., *Troop Morale and Popular Culture in the British and Dominion Armies 1914–1918* (Oxford, 1990).

Fussell, P., *The Great War and Modern Memory* (Oxford, 1977).

Galliher, J. F., Ray, G. and Cook, B., 'Abolition and Reinstatement of Capital Punishment During the Progressive Era and early 20th Century', *Journal of Criminal Law and Criminology*, Vol. 83, No. 3 (USA, 1992).

Gammage, D., *The Broken Years: Australian Soldiers in the Great War* (Canberra, 1974)

Gilbert, M., *First World War* (London, 1994).

Hichberger, J.W.M., *Images of the Army; The Military in British Art 1815–1914* (Manchester, 1988).

Hickman, M., *Religion, Class and Identity* (Aldershot, 1995).

Hogg, I. V., *The Guns 1914–18* (London, 1973).

Hughes, C., 'The New Armies' in Beckett, I. F. W. and Simpson, K. (eds), *A Nation in Arms. A Social Study of the British Army in the First World War* (Manchester, 1985).

Hynes, S., *A War Imagined* (London, 1992).

Jahr, C., *Gewöhnliche Soldaten. Desertion und Deserteure im deutschen und britischen Heer 1914–1918* (Vandenhoeck & Ruprecht, Göttingen, 1998)

James, E. A., *British Regiments 1914–1918* (London, 1993).

James, L., *Mutiny* (London, 1987).

Jeffrey, K., 'The Post War Army' in I. F. W. Beckett and K. Simpson, *A Nation In Arms* (Manchester, 1985).

Joll, J., *1914 – The Unspoken Assumptions* (London, 1968).

Joll, J., *The Origins of the First World War* (Harlow, 1984).

Joll, J.,*Europe Since 1870* (Harmondsworth, 1990).

Keating, J., 'The Tyneside Irish Brigade' in Lavery, F. (ed.), *Great Irishmen in War and Politics* (London, 1920)

Keegan, J., *The Face of Battle* (Harmondsworth, 1976).

Keegan, J., *A History of Warfare* (London, 1993).

Killingray, D., 'Race and Rank in the British Army in the Twentieth

Century' in *Ethnic and Racial Studies*, Vol. 10, No. 3 (July 1987).

Lavery, F. (ed.), *Great Irishmen in War and Politics* (London, 1920).

Leed, E. J., *No Man's Land: Combat and Identity in World War One* (Cambridge,1979).

Leese, P. J., *A Social and Cultural History of Shell-shock with particular reference to the experience of British soldiers before during and after theGreat War*, unpublished PhD thesis, Open University (1989).

MacDonald, L., *1915 The Death of Innocence* (London, 1993).

MacDougall, H. A., *Racial Myth in English History: Trojans, Teutons and Anglo-Saxons* (Montreal, 1982).

Marwick, A., *The Deluge, Second Edition* (Basingstoke, 1991).

Middlebrook, M., and M., *The Somme Battlefields* (Harmondsworth, 1994).

Metcalf, T. R., *Ideologies of the Raj* (Cambridge, 1997).

Millett, A. R., and Murray, W. (eds), *Military Effectiveness: Volume 1 – The First World War* (Boston, 1988).

Moran, Lord, *The Anatomy of Courage* (London, 1966).

Moore W., *See How They Ran* (London, 1970).

Moore, W., *The Thin Yellow Line* (London, 1974).

Moorehead, A., *Gallipoli* (Ware, 1997).

Morton, D., 'The Supreme Penalty: Canadian Deaths by Firing Squad in the First World War' in *Queen's Quarterly*, No. 79 (1972).

Morton, D., *When Your Number's Up: The Canadian Soldier in the First World War* (Toronto, 1993).

Offenstadt, N., 'La rehabilitation des 'fusilles pour l'example' de la Grande Guerre' in *Revue d'histoire moderne et contemporaine*, Vol. 44, No. 1 (1997).

Oram, G., *Death Sentences passed by military courts of the British Army 1914–1924* (London, 1998).

Packenham, T., *The Boer War* (London, 1979).

Pedroncini, G., *Les Mutineries de 1917* (Paris, 1967).

Pick, D., *Faces of Degeneration* (Cambridge, 1989).

Pick, D., *War Machine* (London, 1993).

Porter, R. (ed.), *Myths of the English* (Cambridge 1993).

Pugsley, C., *On the Fringe of Hell* (Auckland, 1991).

Putkowski, J. and Sykes, J., *Shot at Dawn* (Barnsley, 1989).

Radzinowicz, L. and Hood, R., *A History of English Criminal Law, Volume 5,*'The Emergence of Penal Policy' (London, 1986).

Searle, G. R., *Eugenics and Politics in Britain 1900–1914* (Leyden, 1976).

Simkins, P., 'The Four Armies 1914–1918' in Chandler, D. and Beckett, I. F. W. (eds), *The Oxford History of the British Army* (Oxford, 1996).

Simpson, K., 'The Officers' in Beckett, I. F. W. and Simpson, K. (eds), *A Nation in Arms. A Social Study of the British Army in the First World War* (Manchester, 1985).

Simon, B. and Bradley, I. (eds), *The Victorian Public School* (Dublin, 1975).

Smith, L. V., 'The Disciplinary Dilemna of French Military Justice: The Case of The Fifth Division D'Infanterie' in *Journal of Military History*, Vol. 55 (Jan.1991).

Smith, L. V., *Between Mutiny and*

Obedience: The Case of the French Fifth Infantry Division During World War I (Princeton, 1994).

Smith, L. V., 'War and 'Politics': The French Army Mutinies of 1917' in *War in History*, Vol. 2, No. 2 (1995).

Stevenson, J., *British Society 1914–45* (Harmondsworth, 1990).

Stewart, A. T. Q., *The Ulster Crisis: Resistance to Home Rule 1912–1914* (Belfast, 1997).

Stone, M., 'Shell-shock and the Psychologists' in Bynum, W. F., Porter, R. and Shepherd, M. (eds), *Anatomy of Madness*, Volume II (London, 1985).

Strachan, H., *The Politics of the British Army* (Oxford, 1997).

Surridge, K., 'All you soldiers are what we call pro-Boer': The Military Critique of the South African War, 1899–1902' in *History* (Oct. 1997).

Taylor, A.J.P., *The First World War* (Harmondsworth, 1963).

Terraine, J., *Douglas Haig: The Educated Soldier* (London, 1963).

Terraine, J., *The Great War* (Ware, 1997).

Travers, T. H. E., 'Technology, Tactics, and Morale: Jean de Bloch, The Boer War, and British Military Theory, 1900–1914' in *Journal of Modern History*, Vol. 51 (June, 1979).

Travers, T. H. E., 'The Hidden Army: Structural Problems in the British Officer Corps, 1900–1918' in *Journal of Contemporary History*, Vol. 17 (1982).

Travers, T. H. E., *The Killing Ground: The British Army and the Emergence of Modern Warfare on the Western Front 1900–1918* (London, 1990).

Vance, N., 'The Ideal of Manliness' in Simon, B. and Bradley, I. (eds), *The Victorian Public School* (Dublin, 1975).

Westlake, R., *British Battalions on the Somme* (London, 1994).

Whalen, R. W., *Bitter Wounds: German Victims of the Great War 1914–1939* (London, 1984).

Wilson, T., *The Myriad Faces of War: Britain and the Great War 1914–1918* (Cambridge, 1986).

Winter, D., *Haig's Command* (Harmondsworth, 1991).

Winter, J. M., 'The Impact of the First World War on Civilian Health in Britain' in *Economic History Review*, Volume 30, Number 3 (1977).

Winter, J. M., 'Britain's Lost Generation of the First World War' in *Population Studies*, Volume 31 (1977).

Winter, J. M., 'Military Fitness and Civilian Health in Britain During the First World War' in *Journal of Contemporary History*, Volume 15 (1980).

Winter, J. M., *The Great War and the British People* (London, 1986).

Woodward, D., *Armies of the World 1854–1914* (London, 1978).

Index

140